Elasticsearch for Hadoop

Integrate Elasticsearch into Hadoop to effectively
visualize and analyze your data

Vishal Shukla

[PACKT]
PUBLISHING

open source
community experience distilled

BIRMINGHAM - MUMBAI

Elasticsearch for Hadoop

First published: October 2015

Production reference: 1201015

Published by Packt Publishing Ltd.
Livery Place
35 Livery Street
Birmingham B3 2PB, UK.

ISBN 978-1-78528-899-9

www.packtpub.com

Credits

Author
Vishal Shukla

Reviewers
Vincent Behar

Elias Abou Haydar

Yi Wang

Acquisition Editors
Vivek Anantharaman

Larissa Pinto

Content Development Editor
Pooja Mhapsekar

Technical Editor
Siddhesh Ghadi

Copy Editor
Relin Hedly

Project Coordinator
Suzanne Coutinho

Proofreader
Safis Editing

Indexer
Mariammal Chettiyar

Graphics
Disha Haria

Production Coordinator
Nilesh R. Mohite

Cover Work
Nilesh R. Mohite

About the Author

Vishal Shukla is the CEO of Brevitaz Systems (http://brevitaz.com) and a technology evangelist at heart. He is a passionate software scientist and a big data expert. Vishal has extensive experience in designing modular enterprise systems. Since his college days (more than 11 years), Vishal has enjoyed coding in JVM-based languages. He also embraces design thinking and sustainable software development. He has vast experience in architecting enterprise systems in various domains. Vishal is deeply interested in technologies related to big data engineering, analytics, and machine learning.

He set up Brevitaz Systems. This company delivers massively scalable and sustainable big data and analytics-based enterprise applications to their global clientele. With varied expertise in big data technologies and architectural acumen, the Brevitaz team successfully developed and re-engineered a number of legacy systems to state-of-the-art scalable systems. Brevitaz has imbibed in its culture agile practices, such as scrum, test-driven development, continuous integration, and continuous delivery, to deliver high-quality products to its clients.

Vishal is a music and art lover. He loves to sing, play musical instruments, draw portraits, and play sports, such as cricket, table tennis, and pool, in his free time.

You can contact Vishal at vishal.shukla@brevitaz.com and on LinkedIn at https://in.linkedin.com/in/vishalshu. You can also follow Vishal on Twitter at @vishal1shukla2.

I would like to express special thanks to my beloved wife, Sweta Bhatt Shukla, and my awaited baby for always encouraging me to go ahead with the book, giving me company during late nights throughout the write-up, and not complaining about my lack of time. My hearty thanks to my sister Krishna Meet Bhavesh Shah and Arpit Panchal for their detailed reviews, invaluable suggestions, and assistance. Heartfelt thanks to my brother and idol, Pranav Shukla, and my family and friends for their continued support and guidance.

I would also like to express my gratitude to my mentors and colleagues, whose interaction transformed me into what I am today. Though everyone's contribution is vital, it is not possible to name them all, so to name a few, I would like to thank Thomas Hirsch, Sven Boeckelmann, Abhay Chrungoo, Nikunj Parmar, Kuntal Shah, Vinit Yadav, Kruti Shukla, Brett Connor, and Lovato Claiton.

About the Reviewers

Vincent Behar is a passionate software developer. He has worked on a search engine, indexing 16 billion web pages. In this big data environment, the tools he used were Hadoop, MapReduce, and Cascading. Vincent has also worked with Elasticsearch in a large multitenant setup, with both ELK stack and specific indexing/searching requirements. Therefore, bringing these two technologies together, along with new frameworks such as Spark, was the next natural step.

Elias Abou Haydar is a data scientist at iGraal in Paris, France. He obtained an MSc in computer science, specializing in distributed systems and algorithms, from the University of Paris Denis Diderot. He was a research intern at LIAFA, CNRS, working on distributed graph algorithms in image segmentation applications. He discovered Elasticsearch during his end-of-course internship and has been passionate about it ever since.

Yi Wang is currently a lead software engineer at Trendalytics, a data analytics start-up. He is responsible for specifying, designing, and implementing data collection, visualization, and analysis pipelines. He holds a master's degree in computer science from Columbia University and a master's degree in physics from Peking University, with a mixed academic background in math, chemistry, and biology.

www.PacktPub.com

Support files, eBooks, discount offers, and more

For support files and downloads related to your book, please visit www.PacktPub.com.

Did you know that Packt offers eBook versions of every book published, with PDF and ePub files available? You can upgrade to the eBook version at www.PacktPub.com and as a print book customer, you are entitled to a discount on the eBook copy. Get in touch with us at service@packtpub.com for more details.

At www.PacktPub.com, you can also read a collection of free technical articles, sign up for a range of free newsletters and receive exclusive discounts and offers on Packt books and eBooks.

https://www2.packtpub.com/books/subscription/packtlib

Do you need instant solutions to your IT questions? PacktLib is Packt's online digital book library. Here, you can search, access, and read Packt's entire library of books.

Why subscribe?

- Fully searchable across every book published by Packt
- Copy and paste, print, and bookmark content
- On demand and accessible via a web browser

Free access for Packt account holders

If you have an account with Packt at www.PacktPub.com, you can use this to access PacktLib today and view 9 entirely free books. Simply use your login credentials for immediate access.

Table of Contents

Preface

The core components of Hadoop have been around from 2004-2006 as MapReduce. Hadoop's ability to scale and process data in a distributed manner has resulted in its broad acceptance across industries. Very large organizations are able to realize the value that Hadoop brings in: crunching terabytes and petabytes of data, ingesting social data, and utilizing commodity hardware to store huge volume of data. However, *big data solutions* must fulfill its appetite for the speed, especially when you query across unstructured data.

This book will introduce you to Elasticsearch, a powerful distributed search and analytics engine, which can make sense of your massive data in real time. Its rich querying capabilities can help in performing complex full-text search, geospatial analysis, and detect anomalies in your data. Elasticsearch-Hadoop, also widely known as ES-Hadoop, is a two-way connector between Elasticsearch and Hadoop. It opens the doors to flow your data easily to and from the Hadoop ecosystem and Elasticsearch. It can flow the streaming data from Apache Storm or Apache Spark to Elasticsearch and let you analyze it in real time.

The aim of the book is to give you practical skills on how you can harness the power of Elasticsearch and Hadoop. I will walk you through the step-by-step process of how to discover your data and find interesting insights out of massive amount of data. You will learn how to integrate Elasticsearch seamlessly with Hadoop ecosystem tools, such as Pig, Hive, Cascading, Apache Storm, and Apache Spark. This book will enable you to use Elasticsearch to build your own analytics dashboard. It will also enable you to use powerful analytics and the visualization platform, Kibana, to give different shapes, size, and colors to your data.

I have chosen interesting datasets to give you the real-world *data exploration* experience. So, you can quickly use these tools and techniques to build your domain-specific solutions. I hope that reading this book turns out to be fun and a great learning experience for you.

What this book covers

Chapter 1, Setting Up Environment, serves as a step-by-step guide to set up your environment, including Java, Hadoop, Elasticsearch, and useful plugins. Test the environment setup by running a WordCount job to import the results to Elasticsearch.

Chapter 2, Getting Started With ES-Hadoop, walks you through how the WordCount job was developed. We will take a look at the real-world problem to solve it better by introducing Elasticsearch to the Hadoop ecosystem.

Chapter 3, Understanding Elasticsearch, provides you detailed understanding on how to use Elasticsearch for full text search and analytics. With practical examples, you will learn indexing, search, and aggregation APIs.

Chapter 4, Visualizing Big Data Using Kibana, introduces Kibana with real-world examples to show how you can give different shapes and colors to your big data. It demonstrates how to discover your data and visualize it in dynamic dashboards.

Chapter 5, Real-Time Analytics, shows how Elasticsearch and Apache Storm can solve your real-time analytics requirements by classifying and streaming tweets data. We will see how to harness Elasticsearch to solve the data mining problem of anomaly detection.

Chapter 6, ES-Hadoop In Production, explains how Elasticsearch and the ES-Hadoop library works in distributed deployments and how to make the best out of it for your needs. It provides you practical skills to tweak configurations for your specific deployment needs. We will have a configuration checklist for production and skills to administer the cluster.

Chapter 7, Integrating with the Hadoop Ecosystem, takes practical examples to show how you can integrate Elasticsearch with Hadoop ecosystem technologies, such as Pig, Hive, Cascading, and Apache Spark.

Appendix, Configurations, contains a list of configuration options for any of the Hadoop ecosystem integrations.

What you need for this book

A major part of the book is focused on practical examples. You can get the maximum out of this book by actually trying out the examples in this book. Throughout the book, you will have specific instructions on how to set up the software and tools required whenever it is needed.

A Linux-based physical or virtualized machine is all you need to for this book. All instructions and examples of the book are tested for the Ubuntu 14.04 distribution. However, these examples should run fine on other Linux flavors and operating systems as well with relevant changes in OS-specific commands. For Windows users, the easiest way would be to set up Ubuntu VM with virtualization tools (such as VirtualBox or VMware).

Who this book is for

This book is targeted at Java developers who have a basic knowledge of Hadoop. No prior Elasticsearch experience is expected.

Conventions

In this book, you will find a number of text styles that distinguish between different kinds of information. Here are some examples of these styles and an explanation of their meaning.

Code words in text, database table names, folder names, filenames, file extensions, pathnames, dummy URLs, user input, and Twitter handles are shown as follows: "We can include other contexts through the use of the `include` directive."

A block of code is set as follows:

```
{
  "properties": {
    "skills": {
      "type": "string",
      "analyzer": "simple"
    }
  }
}
```

When we wish to draw your attention to a particular part of a code block, the relevant lines or items are set in bold:

```
StatusListener listener = new StatusListener() {
public void onStatus(Status status) {
        queue.offer(status);
    }
    …
    …
```

Any command-line input or output is written as follows:
```
SELECT c.city, s.skill, avg(c.experience)
```

New terms and **important words** are shown in bold. Words that you see on the screen, for example, in menus or dialog boxes, appear in the text like this: "Clicking the **Next** button moves you to the next screen."

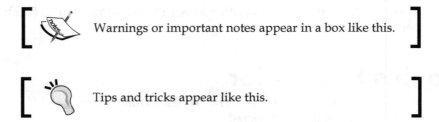

Warnings or important notes appear in a box like this.

Tips and tricks appear like this.

Reader feedback

Feedback from our readers is always welcome. Let us know what you think about this book—what you liked or disliked. Reader feedback is important for us as it helps us develop titles that you will really get the most out of.

To send us general feedback, simply e-mail feedback@packtpub.com, and mention the book's title in the subject of your message.

If there is a topic that you have expertise in and you are interested in either writing or contributing to a book, see our author guide at www.packtpub.com/authors.

Customer support

Now that you are the proud owner of a Packt book, we have a number of things to help you to get the most from your purchase.

Downloading the example code

You can download the example code files from your account at http://www.packtpub.com for all the Packt Publishing books you have purchased. If you purchased this book elsewhere, you can visit http://www.packtpub.com/support and register to have the files e-mailed directly to you.

Downloading the color images of this book

We also provide you with a PDF file that has color images of the screenshots/diagrams used in this book. The color images will help you better understand the changes in the output. You can download this file from http://www.packtpub.com/sites/default/files/downloads/1234OT_ColorImages.pdf.

Errata

Although we have taken every care to ensure the accuracy of our content, mistakes do happen. If you find a mistake in one of our books—maybe a mistake in the text or the code—we would be grateful if you could report this to us. By doing so, you can save other readers from frustration and help us improve subsequent versions of this book. If you find any errata, please report them by visiting http://www.packtpub.com/submit-errata, selecting your book, clicking on the **Errata Submission Form** link, and entering the details of your errata. Once your errata are verified, your submission will be accepted and the errata will be uploaded to our website or added to any list of existing errata under the Errata section of that title.

To view the previously submitted errata, go to https://www.packtpub.com/books/content/support and enter the name of the book in the search field. The required information will appear under the **Errata** section.

Piracy

Piracy of copyrighted material on the Internet is an ongoing problem across all media. At Packt, we take the protection of our copyright and licenses very seriously. If you come across any illegal copies of our works in any form on the Internet, please provide us with the location address or website name immediately so that we can pursue a remedy.

Please contact us at copyright@packtpub.com with a link to the suspected pirated material.

We appreciate your help in protecting our authors and our ability to bring you valuable content.

Questions

If you have a problem with any aspect of this book, you can contact us at questions@packtpub.com, and we will do our best to address the problem.

Setting Up Environment

1

The goal of this book is to get you up and running with ES-Hadoop and enable you to solve real-world analytics problems. To take the first step towards doing this, we will start with setting up Hadoop, Elasticsearch, and related toolsets, which you will use throughout the rest of the book.

We encourage you to try the examples in the book (along with reading) to speed up the learning process.

In this chapter, we will cover the following topics:

- Setting up Hadoop in pseudo-distributed mode
- Setting up Elasticsearch and its related plugins
- Running the `WordCount` example
- Exploring data in Marvel and Head

Setting up Hadoop for Elasticsearch

For our exploration on Hadoop and Elasticsearch, we will use an Ubuntu-based host. However, you may opt to run any other Linux OS and set up Hadoop and Elasticsearch.

Being a Hadoop user, if you already have Hadoop set up in your local machine, you may jump directly to the section, *Setting up Elasticsearch*.

Hadoop supports three cluster modes: the stand-alone mode, the pseudo-distributed mode, and the fully-distributed mode. To make it good enough to walk through the examples of the book, we will consider the pseudo-distributed mode on a Linux operating system. This mode will ensure that without getting into the complexity of setting up so many nodes, we will mirror the components in such a way that they behave no differently to the real production environment. In the pseudo-distributed mode, each component runs on its own JVM process.

Setting up Java

The examples in this book are developed and tested against Oracle Java 1.8. These examples should run fine with other distributions of Java 8 as well.

In order to set up Oracle Java 8, open the terminal and execute the following steps:

1. First, add and update the repository for Java 8 with the following command:

```
$ sudo add-apt-repository ppa:webupd8team/java
$ sudo apt-get update
```

2. Next, install Java 8 and configure the environment variables, as shown in the following command:

```
$ sudo apt-get install oracle-java8-set-default
```

3. Now, verify the installation as follows:

```
$ java -version
```

This should show an output similar to the following code; it may vary a bit based on the exact version:

```
java version "1.8.0_60"

Java(TM) SE Runtime Environment (build 1.8.0_60-b27)

Java HotSpot(TM) 64-Bit Server VM (build 25.60-b23, mixed
mode)
```

Setting up a dedicated user

To ensure that our ES-Hadoop environment is clean and isolated from the rest of the applications and to be able to manage security and permissions easily, we will set up a dedicated user. Perform the following steps:

1. First, add the hadoop group with the following command:

```
$ sudo addgroup hadoop
```

2. Then, add the eshadoop user to the hadoop group, as shown in the following command:

```
$ sudo adduser eshadoop hadoop
```

3. Finally, add the eshadoop user to the sudoers list by adding the user to the sudo group as follows:

```
$ sudo adduser eshadoop sudo
```

Now, you need to relogin with the eshadoop user to execute further steps.

Installing SSH and setting up the certificate

In order to manage nodes, Hadoop requires an SSH access, so let's install and run the SSH. Perform the following steps:

1. First, install ssh with the following command:

   ```
   $ sudo apt-get install ssh
   ```

2. Then, generate a new SSH key pair using the ssh-keygen utility, by using the following command:

   ```
   $ ssh-keygen -t rsa -P ''  -C email@example.com
   ```

    You must use the default settings when asked for **Enter file in which to save the key**. By default, it should generate the key pair under the /home/eshadoop/.ssh folder.

3. Now, confirm the key generation by issuing the following command. This command should display at least a couple of files with id_rsa and id_rsa. pub. We just created an RSA key pair with an empty password so that Hadoop can interact with nodes without the need to enter the passphrase:

   ```
   $ ls -l ~/.ssh
   ```

4. To enable the SSH access to your local machine, you need to specify that the newly generated public key is an authorized key to log in using the following command:

   ```
   $ cat ~/.ssh/id_rsa.pub >> ~/.ssh/authorized_keys
   ```

5. Finally, do not forget to test the password-less ssh using the following command:

   ```
   $ ssh localhost
   ```

Downloading Hadoop

Using the following commands, download Hadoop and extract the file to /usr/ local so that it is available for other users as well. Perform the following steps:

1. First, download the Hadoop tarball by running the following command:

   ```
   $ wget http://ftp.wayne.edu/apache/hadoop/common/hadoop-2.6.0/
   hadoop-2.6.0.tar.gz
   ```

2. Next, extract the tarball to the /usr/local directory with the following command:

   ```
   $ sudo tar vxzf hadoop-2.6.0.tar.gz -C /usr/local
   ```

Note that extracting it to /usr/local will affect other users as well. In other words, it will be available to other users as well, assuming that appropriate permissions are provided for the directory.

3. Now, rename the Hadoop directory using the following command:

```
$ cd /usr/local
$ sudo mv hadoop-2.6.0 hadoop
```

4. Finally, change the owner of all the files to the eshadoop user and the hadoop group with the following command:

```
$ sudo chown -R eshadoop:hadoop hadoop
```

Setting up environment variables

The next step is to set up environment variables. You can do so by exporting the required variables to the .bashrc file for the user.

Open the .bashrc file using any editor of your choice, then add the following export declarations to set up our environment variables:

```
#Set JAVA_HOME
export JAVA_HOME=/usr/lib/jvm/java-8-oracle

#Set Hadoop related environment variable
export HADOOP_INSTALL=/usr/local/hadoop

#Add bin and sbin directory to PATH
export PATH=$PATH:$HADOOP_INSTALL/bin
export PATH=$PATH:$HADOOP_INSTALL/sbin

#Set few more Hadoop related environment variable
export HADOOP_MAPRED_HOME=$HADOOP_INSTALL
export HADOOP_COMMON_HOME=$HADOOP_INSTALL
export HADOOP_HDFS_HOME=$HADOOP_INSTALL
export YARN_HOME=$HADOOP_INSTALL
export HADOOP_COMMON_LIB_NATIVE_DIR=$HADOOP_INSTALL/lib/native
export HADOOP_OPTS="-Djava.library.path=$HADOOP_INSTALL/lib"
```

Once you have saved the .bashrc file, you can relogin to have your new environment variables visible, or you can source the .bashrc file using the following command:

```
$ source ~/.bashrc
```

Configuring Hadoop

Now, we need to set up the JAVA_HOME environment variable in the hadoop-env.sh file that is used by Hadoop. You can find it in $HADOOP_INSTALL/etc/hadoop.

Next, change the JAVA_HOME path to reflect to your Java installation directory. On my machine, it looks similar to the following:

```
$ export JAVA_HOME=/usr/lib/jvm/java-8-oracle
```

Now, let's relogin and confirm the configuration using the following command:

```
$ hadoop version
```

As you know, we will set up our Hadoop environment in a pseudo-distributed mode. In this mode, each Hadoop daemon runs in a separate Java process. The next step is to configure these daemons. So, let's switch to the following folder that contains all the Hadoop configuration files:

```
$ cd $HADOOP_INSTALL/etc/hadoop
```

Configuring core-site.xml

The configuration of core-site.xml will set up the temporary directory for Hadoop and the default filesystem. In our case, the default filesystem refers to the NameNode. Let's change the content of the <configuration> section of core-site.xml so that it looks similar to the following code:

```
<configuration>
<property>
  <name>hadoop.tmp.dir</name>
  <value>/home/eshadoop/hdfs/tmp</value>
  <description>A base for other temporary
directories.</description>
 </property>
<property>
   <name>fs.default.name</name>
   <value>hdfs://localhost:9000</value>
</property>
</configuration>
```

Configuring hdfs-site.xml

Now, we will configure the replication factor for HDFS files. To set the replication to 1, change the content of the `<configuration>` section of `hdfs-site.xml` so that it looks similar to the following code:

```
<configuration>
   <property>
   <name>dfs.replication</name>
   <value>1</value>
 </property>
</configuration>
```

> We will run Hadoop in the pseudo-distributed mode. In order to do this, we need to configure the YARN resource manager. YARN handles the resource management and scheduling responsibilities in the Hadoop cluster so that the data processing and data storage components can focus on their respective tasks.

Configuring yarn-site.xml

Configure `yarn-site.xml` in order to configure the auxiliary service name and classes, as shown in the following code:

```
<configuration>
<property>
   <name>yarn.nodemanager.aux-services</name>
   <value>mapreduce_shuffle</value>
</property>
<property>
   <name>yarn.nodemanager.aux-
services.mapreduce.shuffle.class</name>
   <value>org.apache.hadoop.mapred.ShuffleHandler</value>
</property>
</configuration>
```

Configuring mapred-site.xml

Hadoop provides `mapred-site.xml.template`, which you can rename to `mapred-site.xml` and change the content of the `<configuration>` section to the following code; this will ensure that the MapReduce jobs run on YARN as opposed to running them in-process locally:

```
<configuration>
   <property>
```

```
        <name>mapred.job.tracker</name>
        <value>yarn</value>
    </property>
</configuration>
```

The format distributed filesystem

We have already configured all the Hadoop daemons, including HDFS, YARN, and the JobTracker. You may already be aware that HDFS relies on NameNode and DataNodes. NameNode contains the storage-related metadata, whereas DataNode stores the real data in the form of blocks. When you set up your Hadoop cluster, it is required to format NameNode before you can start using HDFS. We can do so with the following command:

```
$ hadoop namenode -format
```

> If you were already using the data nodes of HDFS, do not format the name node unless you know what you are doing. When you format NameNode, you will lose all the storage metadata, just as the blocks are distributed among DataNodes. This means that although you didn't physically remove the data from DataNodes, the data will be inaccessible to you. Therefore, it is always good to remove the data in DataNodes when you format the NameNode.

Starting Hadoop daemons

Now, we have all the prerequisites set up along with all the Hadoop daemons. In order to run our first MapReduce job, we need all the required Hadoop daemons running.

Let's start with HDFS using the following command. This command starts the NameNode, SecondaryNameNode, and DataNode daemons:

```
$ start-dfs.sh
```

The next step is to start the YARN resource manager using the following command (YARN will start the ResourceManager and NodeManager daemons):

```
$ start-yarn.sh
```

If the preceding two commands were successful in starting HDFS and YARN, you should be able to check the running daemons using the `jps` tool (this tool lists the running JVM process on your machine):

```
$ jps
```

If everything worked successfully, you should see the following services running:

```
13386 SecondaryNameNode
13059 NameNode
13179 DataNode
17490 Jps
13649 NodeManager
13528 ResourceManager
```

Setting up Elasticsearch

In this section, we will download and configure the Elasticsearch server and install the Elasticsearch Head and Marvel plugins.

Downloading Elasticsearch

To download Elasticsearch, perform the following steps:

1. First, download Elasticsearch using the following command:

    ```
    $ wget https://download.elastic.co/elasticsearch/elasticsearch/
    elasticsearch-1.7.1.tar.gz
    ```

2. Once the file is downloaded, extract it to /usr/local and rename it with a convenient name, using the following command:

    ```
    $ sudo tar -xvzf elasticsearch-1.7.1.tar.gz -C /usr/local
    ```

    ```
    $ sudo mv /usr/local/elasticsearch-1.7.1 /usr/local/elasticsearch
    ```

3. Then, set the eshadoop user as the owner of the directory as follows:

    ```
    $ sudo chown -R eshadoop:hadoop /usr/local/elasticsearch
    ```

Configuring Elasticsearch

The Elasticsearch configuration file, elasticsearch.yml, can be located in the config folder under the Elasticsearch home directory. Open the elasticsearch.yml file in the editor of your choice by using the following command:

```
$ cd /usr/local/elasticsearch
```

```
$ vi config/elasticsearch.yml
```

Uncomment the line with the cluster.name key from the elasticsearch.yml file and change the cluster name, as shown in the following code:

```
cluster.name:eshadoopcluster
```

Similarly, uncomment the line with the node.name key and change the value as follows:

```
node.name:"ES Hadoop Node"
```

Elasticsearch comes with a decent default configuration to let you start the nodes with zero additional configurations. In a production environment and even in a development environment, sometimes it may be desirable to tweak some configurations.

By default, Elasticsearch assigns the node name from the randomly picked Marvel character name from a list of 3,000 names. The default cluster name assigned to the node is elasticsearch. With the default configurations of ES nodes in the same network and the same cluster name, Elasticsearch will synchronize the data between the nodes. This may be unwanted if each developer is looking for an isolated ES server setup. It's always good to specify cluster.name and node.name to avoid unwanted surprises.

You can change the defaults for configurations starting with path.*. To set up the directories that store the server data, to locate paths section, and to uncomment the highlighted paths and changes, use the following code:

```
########################## paths ###########################
# Path to directory containing configuration (this file and
logging.yml):
#
path.conf: /usr/local/elasticsearch/config

# Path to directory where to store index data allocated for this
node.
#
# Can optionally include more than one location, causing data to
be striped across
# the locations (a la RAID 0) on a file level, favouring locations
with most free
# space on creation.
path.data: /usr/local/elasticsearch/data


# Path to temporary files:
#
path.work: /usr/local/elasticsearch/work

# Path to log files:
#
path.logs: /usr/local/elasticsearch/logs
```

It's important to choose the location of `path.data` wisely. In production, you should make sure that this path doesn't exist in the Elasticsearch installation directory in order to avoid accidently overwriting or deleting the data when upgrading Elasticsearch.

Installing Elasticsearch's Head plugin

Elasticsearch provides a plugin utility to install the Elasticsearch plugins. Execute the following command to install the Head plugin:

```
$ bin/plugin -install mobz/elasticsearch-head


-> Installing mobz/elasticsearch-head...
Trying https://github.com/mobz/elasticsearch-head/archive/master.zip...
Downloading ................................................................
.........................................................................
.........................................................................
.........................................................................
.........................................................................
.........................................................................
.........................................................................
.........................................................DONE
Installed mobz/elasticsearch-head into /usr/local /elasticsearch/plugins/
head
Identified as a _site plugin, moving to _site structure ...
```

As indicated by the console output, the plugin is successfully installed in the default plugins directory under the Elasticsearch home. You can access the head plugin at `http://localhost:9200/_plugin/head/`.

Installing the Marvel plugin

Now, let's install the Marvel plugin using a similar command:

```
$ bin/plugin -i elasticsearch/marvel/latest


-> Installing elasticsearch/marvel/latest...
Trying http://download.elasticsearch.org/elasticsearch/marvel/marvel-
latest.zip...
```

```
Downloading .....................................................
...............................................................
...............................................................
...............................................................
.................................DONE
```

```
Installed elasticsearch/marvel/latest into /usr/local/elasticsearch/
plugins/marvel
```

Running and testing

Finally, start Elasticsearch using the following command:

```
$ ./bin/elasticsearch
```

We will then get the following log:

```
[2015-05-13 21:59:37,344][INFO ][node                     ] [ES Hadoop
Node] version[1.5.1], pid[3822], build[5e38401/2015-04-09T13:41:35Z]

[2015-05-13 21:59:37,346][INFO ][node                     ] [ES Hadoop
Node] initializing ...

[2015-05-13 21:59:37,358][INFO ][plugins                  ] [ES Hadoop
Node] loaded [marvel], sites [marvel, head]

[2015-05-13 21:59:39,956][INFO ][node                     ] [ES Hadoop
Node] initialized

[2015-05-13 21:59:39,959][INFO ][node                     ] [ES Hadoop
Node] starting ...

[2015-05-13 21:59:40,133][INFO ][transport                ] [ES Hadoop
Node] bound_address {inet[/0:0:0:0:0:0:0:0:9300]}, publish_address
{inet[/10.0.2.15:9300]}

[2015-05-13 21:59:40,159][INFO ][discovery                ] [ES Hadoop
Node] eshadoopcluster/_bzqXWbLSXKXWpafHaLyRA

[2015-05-13 21:59:43,941][INFO ][cluster.service          ] [ES Hadoop
Node] new_master [ES Hadoop Node][_bzqXWbLSXKXWpafHaLyRA][eshadoop]
[inet[/10.0.2.15:9300]], reason: zen-disco-join (elected_as_master)

[2015-05-13 21:59:43,989][INFO ][http                     ] [ES Hadoop
Node] bound_address {inet[/0:0:0:0:0:0:0:0:9200]}, publish_address
{inet[/10.0.2.15:9200]}

[2015-05-13 21:59:43,989][INFO ][node                     ] [ES Hadoop
Node] started

[2015-05-13 21:59:44,026][INFO ][gateway                  ] [ES Hadoop
Node] recovered [0] indices into cluster_state
```

```
[2015-05-13 22:00:00,707][INFO ][cluster.metadata         ] [ES Hadoop
Node] [.marvel-2015.05.13] creating index, cause [auto(bulk api)],
templates [marvel], shards [1]/[1], mappings [indices_stats, cluster_
stats, node_stats, shard_event, node_event, index_event, index_stats,
_default_, cluster_state, cluster_event, routing_event]
[2015-05-13 22:00:01,421][INFO ][cluster.metadata         ] [ES Hadoop
Node] [.marvel-2015.05.13] update_mapping [node_stats] (dynamic)
```

The startup logs will give you some useful hints as to what is going on. By default, Elasticsearch uses the transport ports from 9200 to 9299 for HTTP, allocating the first port that is available for the node. In the highlighted output, you can also see that it binds to the port 9300 as well. Elasticsearch uses the port range from 9300 to 9399 for an internal node-to-node communication or when communicating using the Java client. It can use the zen multicast or the unicast ping discovery to find other nodes in the cluster with multicast as the default. We will understand more about these discovery nodes in later chapters.

Running the WordCount example

Now that we have got our ES-Hadoop environment tested and running, we are all set to run our first WordCount example. In the Hadoop world, WordCount has made its place to replace the HelloWorld program, hasn't it?

Getting the examples and building the job JAR file

You can download the examples in the book from https://github.com/ vishalbrevitaz/eshadoop/tree/master/ch01. Once you have got the source code, you can build the JAR file for this chapter using the steps mentioned in the readme file in the source code zip. The build process should generate a ch01-0.0.1-job.jar file under the <SOURCE_CODE_BASE_DIR>/ch01/target directory.

Importing the test file to HDFS

For our WordCount example, you can use any text file of your choice. To explain the example, we will use the sample.txt file that is part of the source zip. Perform the following steps:

1. First, let's create a nice directory structure in HDFS to manage our input files with the following command:

   ```
   $ hadoop fs -mkdir /input
   $ hadoop fs -mkdir /input/ch01
   ```

2. Next, upload the `sample.txt` file to HDFS at the desired location, by using the following command:

```
$ hadoop fs -put data/ch01/sample.txt /input/ch01/sample.txt
```

3. Now, verify that the file is successfully imported to HDFS by using the following command:

```
$ hadoop fs -ls /input/ch01
```

Finally, when you execute the preceding command, it should show an output similar to the following code:

```
Found 1 items
-rw-r--r--   1 eshadoop supergroup       2803 2015-05-10 15:18 /
input/ch01/sample.txt
```

Running our first job

We are ready with the job JAR file; its sample file is imported to HDFS. Point your terminal to the `<SOURCE_CODE_BASE_DIR>/ch01/target` directory and run the following command:

```
$ hadoop jar ch01-0.0.1-job.jar /input/ch01/sample.txt
```

Now you'll get the following output:

```
15/05/10 15:21:33 INFO client.RMProxy: Connecting to ResourceManager at
/0.0.0.0:8032

15/05/10 15:21:34 WARN mr.EsOutputFormat: Speculative execution enabled
for reducer - consider disabling it to prevent data corruption

15/05/10 15:21:34 INFO util.Version: Elasticsearch Hadoop v2.0.2
[ca81ff6732]

15/05/10 15:21:34 INFO mr.EsOutputFormat: Writing to [eshadoop/wordcount]

15/05/10 15:21:35 WARN mapreduce.JobSubmitter: Hadoop command-line option
parsing not performed. Implement the Tool interface and execute your
application with ToolRunner to remedy this.

15/05/10 15:21:41 INFO input.FileInputFormat: Total input paths to
process : 1

15/05/10 15:21:42 INFO mapreduce.JobSubmitter: number of splits:1

15/05/10 15:21:42 INFO mapreduce.JobSubmitter: Submitting tokens for job:
job_1431251282365_0002

15/05/10 15:21:42 INFO impl.YarnClientImpl: Submitted application
application_1431251282365_0002

15/05/10 15:21:42 INFO mapreduce.Job: The url to track the job: http://
eshadoop:8088/proxy/application_1431251282365_0002/
```

```
15/05/10 15:21:42 INFO mapreduce.Job: Running job: job_1431251282365_0002
15/05/10 15:21:54 INFO mapreduce.Job: Job job_1431251282365_0002 running
in uber mode : false
15/05/10 15:21:54 INFO mapreduce.Job:  map 0% reduce 0%
15/05/10 15:22:01 INFO mapreduce.Job:  map 100% reduce 0%
15/05/10 15:22:09 INFO mapreduce.Job:  map 100% reduce 100%
15/05/10 15:22:10 INFO mapreduce.Job: Job job_1431251282365_0002
completed successfully
...

...

...

  Elasticsearch Hadoop Counters
    Bulk Retries=0
    Bulk Retries Total Time(ms)=0
    Bulk Total=1
    Bulk Total Time(ms)=48
    Bytes Accepted=9655
    Bytes Received=4000
    Bytes Retried=0
    Bytes Sent=9655
    Documents Accepted=232
    Documents Received=0
    Documents Retried=0
    Documents Sent=232
    Network Retries=0
    Network Total Time(ms)=84
    Node Retries=0
    Scroll Total=0
    Scroll Total Time(ms)=0
```

Downloading the example code

You can download the example code files for all
Packt books you have purchased from your account
at http://www.packtpub.com. If you purchased
this book elsewhere, you can visit http://www.
packtpub.com/support and register to have the
files e-mailed directly to you.

We just executed our first Hadoop MapReduce job that uses and imports data to Elasticsearch. This MapReduce job simply outputs the count of each word in the Mapper phase, and Reducer calculates the sum of all the counts for each word. We will dig into greater details of how exactly this WordCount program is developed in the next chapter. The console output of the job displays the useful log information to indicate the progress of the job execution. It also displays the *ES-Hadoop counters* that provide some handy information about the amount of data and documents being sent and received, the number of retries, the time taken, and so on. If you have used the `sample.txt` file provided in the source zip, you will be able to see that the job found 232 unique words and all of them are pushed as the Elasticsearch document. In the next section, we will examine these documents with the Elasticsearch Head and Marvel plugin that we already installed in Elasticsearch. Note that you can also track the status of your ES-Hadoop MapReduce jobs, similar to any other Hadoop jobs, in the job tracker. In our setup, you can access the job tracker at `http://localhost:8088/cluster`.

Exploring data in Head and Marvel

In the previous section, we set up a couple of plugins: Head and Marvel. In this section, we will have a bird's eye view of how to use these plugins to explore the Elasticsearch documents that we just imported by running the ES-Hadoop MapReduce job.

Viewing data in Head

The Elasticsearch Head plugin provides a simple web frontend to visualize the Elasticsearch indices, cluster, node health, and statistics. It provides an easy-to-use interface to explore index, types, and documents with the query building interface. It also allows you to view the documents of Elasticsearch in a table-like structure as well, which can be quite handy for users coming from the RDBMS background.

Here is how the **Elasticsearch** Head home page looks when you open `http://localhost:9200/_plugin/head`.

The following image shows the home page of the **Elasticsearch** Head plugin:

You will get a quick insight into your cluster from the preceding screenshot, such as what is cluster health is (*Green*, *Yellow*, or *Red*); how the shards are allocated to different nodes, which indices exist in the cluster, what the size is of each index, and so on. For example, in the preceding screenshot, we can see two indices: **.marvel-2015.05.10** and **eshadoop**. You may be surprised that we never created an index with the name of **.marvel-2015.05.10**. You can ignore this index for the time being; we will take a brief look at it in the next subsection.

Let's go back to our `WordCount` example. You can see that the document count for the **eshadoop** index in the preceding screenshot exactly matches with the number of documents metric indicated by the MapReduce job output that we saw in the last section.

The following diagram shows the **Browser** tab of the Elasticsearch Head plugin:

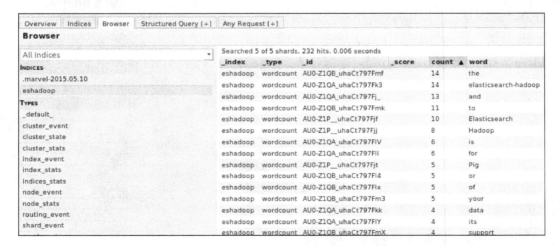

To take a look at the documents, navigate to the **Browser** tab. You can see that the screen is similar to the one shown in the preceding screenshot. You can click on the **eshadoop** index on the left-hand side under the **Indices** heading and sort the results by count to see the relevant documents. You can also see that the output of the MapReduce job is pushed directly to Elasticsearch. Further more, you can see the ES document fields, such as _index, _type, _id, and _score, along with the fields that we are interested in **word** and **count**. You may want to sort the results based on **count** by clicking on the **count** column to see the most frequent words in the sample.txt file.

Using the Marvel dashboard

Marvel is a monitoring dashboard for real-time and historical analysis that is built on top of Kibana: a data visualization tool for ES-Hadoop. This dashboard provides, insight into the different metrics of the node, JVM, and ES-Hadoop internals. To open the Marvel dashboard, refer to your browser at http://localhost:9200/_plugin/marvel/.

The following screenshot gives you an overview of the Marvel dashboard:

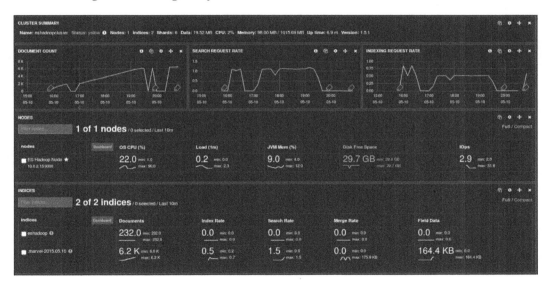

You can see the different real-time metrics for your cluster, nodes, and indices. You can visualize the trends of the document count, search, and the indexing request rates in a graphical way. This kind of visualization may be helpful to get a quick insight into the usage pattern of the index and find out the candidates for the purpose of performance optimization. It displays the vital monitoring stats, such as the CPU usage, the load, the JVM memory usage, the free disk space, and so on. You can also filter by time range in the top-right corner to use the dashboard for historical analysis. Marvel stores these historical data in a separate daily rolling index with a name pattern, such as `.marvel-XXX`.

Exploring the data in Sense

Sense is a plugin embedded in Marvel to provide a seamless and easy-to-use REST API client for the ES-Hadoop server. It is Elasticsearch-aware and frees you from memorizing the ES-Hadoop query syntaxes by providing autosuggestions. It also helps by indicating the typo or syntax errors.

To open the Sense user interface, open `http://localhost:9200/_plugin/marvel/sense/index.html` in your browser.

The following screenshot shows the query interface of Sense:

Now, let's find out the documents imported in the `eshadoop` index by executing the `match_all` query.

Then, use the following query in the query panel on the left-hand side in the sense interface:

```
GET eshadoop/_search
{
    "query": {
        "match_all":{}
    }
}
```

Finally, click on the **Send request** button to execute the query and obtain the results.

 You can point to different Elasticsearch servers if you wish by changing the `server` field at the top.

Summary

In this chapter, we started by checking the prerequisites for how to install Hadoop and configured Hadoop in the pseudo-distributed mode. Then, we got the Elasticsearch server up and running and understood the basic configurations of Elasticsearch. We learned how to install the Elasticsearch plugins. We imported the sample file for the `WordCount` example to HDFS and successfully ran our first Hadoop MapReduce job that uses ES-Hadoop to get the data to Elasticsearch. Then we learned how to use the Head and Marvel plugins to explore documents in Elasticsearch.

With our environment and the required tools set up with a basic understanding, we are all set to have a hands-on experience of how to write MapReduce jobs that use ES-Hadoop. In the next chapter, we will take a look at how the WordCount job is developed. We will also develop a couple of jobs for real-world scenarios that will write and read data to and from HDFS and Elasticsearch.

2
Getting Started with ES-Hadoop

Hadoop provides you with a batch-oriented distributed storage and a computing engine. Elasticsearch is a full-text search engine with rich aggregation capabilities. Getting the data from Hadoop to Elasticsearch can open doors to run some data discovery tools to find out interesting patterns and perform full-text search or geospatial analytics. ES-Hadoop is a library that bridges Hadoop with Elasticsearch. The goal of this book is to get you up-and-running with ES-Hadoop and enable you to solve real-world analytics problems.

Our goal in this chapter is to develop MapReduce jobs to write/read the data to/from Elasticsearch. You probably already know how to write basic MapReduce jobs using Hadoop that writes its output to HDFS. ES-Hadoop is a connector library that provides a dedicated `InputFormat` and `OutputFormat` that you can use to read/write data from/to Elasticsearch in Hadoop jobs. To take the first step in this direction, we will start with how to set up Hadoop, Elasticsearch, and the related toolsets, which you will use throughout the rest of the book.

We encourage you to try the examples in the book to speed up the learning process.

We will cover the following topics in this chapter:

- Understanding the `WordCount` program
- Going real—network monitoring data
- Writing a network logs mapper job
- Getting data from Elasticsearch to HDFS

Understanding the WordCount program

In the previous chapter, we downloaded and ran our first Hadoop MapReduce job that used the ES-Hadoop library. Let's get inside the WordCount job to understand how it is developed.

Understanding Mapper

Here is how `WordsMapper.java` looks:

```
package com.packtpub.esh;

import org.apache.hadoop.io.IntWritable;
import org.apache.hadoop.io.Text;
import org.apache.hadoop.mapreduce.Mapper;

import java.io.IOException;
import java.util.StringTokenizer;

public class WordsMapper extends Mapper<Object, Text, Text,
IntWritable> {

  private final static IntWritable one = new IntWritable(1);

  public void map(Object key, Text value, Context context)  throws
IOException, InterruptedException {
    StringTokenizer itr = new StringTokenizer(value.toString());

    while (itr.hasMoreTokens()) {
          Text word = new Text();
      word.set(itr.nextToken());
      context.write(word, one);
    }
  }
}
```

To all the MapReduce developers, this `Mapper` is very well known and trivial. We will get the input line in the `value` and tokenize it with white space to extract word tokens. For each word, we will then write a count of 1 with the `word` as a key. This is no different than other `WordsMapper` you may have come across so far.

Understanding the reducer

To help you understand the reducer better, let's understand the input that is provided to it. We also have to understand what it is supposed to populate in the context.

We are pretty familiar with the `Mapper` class used for the `WordCount` program. The reducer is provided with all the buckets that contains the same `word` as a key; again this is no different than the conventional `MapReduce` program. When the job gets executed, we want the Elasticsearch index to be populated with the words and its respective counts.

 We have dedicated the next chapter solely to understand Elasticsearch in depth. What is important for you to know as of now is that you can index and read data from Elasticsearch. The unit of these operations is called as *Document*. This is just a JSON object that can have fields and values.

We want the Elasticsearch document to look similar to the following JSON structure:

```
{
  "word":"Elasticsearch-hadoop",
  "count":14
}
```

We need to represent this document in Java. This should be written to the `Context` object. We can easily map the key/value-based JSON document format to the `MapWritable` class. The keys of `MapWriteable` entries will represent the JSON field key, and the values will represent the respective JSON field value. In the JSON example we saw earlier, `word` and `count` becomes the keys of `MapWritable`.

Once the reducer is run and the context output is generated, it is transformed into the JSON format and passed to the RESTful endpoint of Elasticsearch for indexing as the bulk indexing request.

Let's take a look at how the `WordsReducer` class looks in the WordCount job:

```
package com.packtpub.esh;

import org.apache.hadoop.io.IntWritable;
import org.apache.hadoop.io.MapWritable;
import org.apache.hadoop.io.Text;
import org.apache.hadoop.mapreduce.Reducer;

import java.io.IOException;
```

```
public class WordsReducer extends Reducer<Text,IntWritable,Text,MapWr
itable> {

  @Override
  public void reduce(Text key, Iterable<IntWritable> values,
Context context) throws IOException, InterruptedException {
    // This represents our ES document
      MapWritable result = new MapWritable();
    int sum = 0;
    for (IntWritable val : values) {
      sum += val.get();
    }
      // Add "word" field to ES document
    result.put(new Text("word"), key);
      // Add "count" field to ES document
    result.put(new Text("count"), new IntWritable(sum));
    context.write(key, result);
  }

}
```

`WordsReducer` implements the `Reducer` interface with the input key value types as `<Text, Iterable<IntWritable>>` and the output types as `<Text, MapWritable>`. To implement the `reduce` method, we iterated through all the values for `key` to derive the final `sum` value. The final `sum` value and `key` are added in the newly constructed `MapWritable` object. Finally, the `result` is written to the `context` for further processing.

Understanding the driver

We need one final component to drive the job. Let's call this component as `Driver`. This component is responsible for providing job configurations, such as which Elasticsearch nodes and index to point to. It also performs the plumbing work for the job, such as which `Mapper` and `Reducer` class should be used and what their input and output specifications are, including formats and paths.

Here is the `Driver.java` file:

```
import org.apache.hadoop.conf.Configuration;
import org.apache.hadoop.fs.Path;
import org.apache.hadoop.io.IntWritable;
import org.apache.hadoop.io.Text;
import org.apache.hadoop.mapreduce.Job;
import org.apache.hadoop.mapreduce.lib.input.FileInputFormat;
import org.elasticsearch.hadoop.mr.EsOutputFormat;
```

```
public class Driver {

  public static void main(String[] args) throws Exception {
    Configuration conf = new Configuration();
        // Elasticsearch Server nodes to point to
    conf.set("es.nodes", "localhost:9200");

        // Elasticsearch index and type name in {indexName}/{typeName}
format
    conf.set("es.resource", "eshadoop/wordcount");
```

First, we created a job instance by providing the Hadoop Configuration object. Many of the ES-Hadoop library behaviour can be customized as per your needs by setting the relevant properties in this Configuration object. For your reference, these configurations are listed in *Appendix, Configurations*. The Configuration object in the preceding example is set with a couple of the most basic configurations: es.nodes and es.resource.

The es.nodes configuration tells the job about the ES nodes that it should connect to. The value of this setting accepts the <HOSTNAME/IP>:<PORT> format. You can pass multiple comma-separated values for this setting. The ES-Hadoop library uses an HTTP REST endpoint to connect with Elasticsearch. It means that we need to use the HTTP port (by default, 9200) for the connection and not the transport port (by default, 9300).

> It is not required to specify all the cluster nodes in the Elasticsearch cluster in the es.nodes setting. The ES-Hadoop library will discover other nodes in the cluster and use them. However, it's better to provide multiple nodes in this configuration to ensure that even if some of the Elasticsearch nodes are down, your job has at least one or a few nodes running to be able to connect to the cluster.

The es.resource setting specifies the target Elasticsearch index and type. This means that the data will be read or written to the index and type specified here. This configuration takes the <index>/<type> format.

> If you are new to Elasticsearch, you will want to know what index and type means. You can think of index as a database schema and type as a table in a relational database. The Elasticsearch document can be thought of as a row in the relational table. We will cover Elasticsearch's index, type, and document in greater detail in the next chapter.

```
    // Create Job instance
    Job job = new Job(conf, "word count");
    // set Driver class
    job.setJarByClass(Driver.class);
    job.setMapperClass(WordsMapper.class);
    job.setReducerClass(WordsReducer.class);
    job.setOutputKeyClass(Text.class);
    job.setOutputValueClass(IntWritable.class);
    // set OutputFormat to EsOutputFormat provided by
Elasticsearch-Hadoop jar
    job.setOutputFormatClass(EsOutputFormat.class);

    FileInputFormat.addInputPath(job, new Path(args[0]));
    System.exit(job.waitForCompletion(true) ? 0 : 1);
  }


}
```

Once the job is created with the required configurations, other job properties are set as typical MapReduce jobs, such as jarByClass, mapperClass, reducerClass, outputKeyClass, and outputValueClass.

The ES-Hadoop library provides a dedicated EsInputFormat and EsOutputFormat. These act as an adapter between the Hadoop and JSON document format expected by Elasticsearch. By default, EsOutputFormat expects the MapWritable object to be written as the output in the context object. EsOutputFormat then converts this MapWritable object to the JSON object.

> You can write the existing JSON String to Elasticsearch with EsOutputFormat without applying any kind of transformation. In order to do this, set the "es.input.json"="yes" parameter. Setting this configuration makes the ES-Hadoop library look for the BytesWritable or Text object to be provided as the job's output. If none of these are found, it expects the class configured as outputValueClass to provide a toString() method that returns the JSON String.

Using the old API – org.apache.hadoop.mapred

If you are still using the old MapReduce API, the ES-Hadoop library fully supports the old Hadoop version as well.

Here is a code snippet showing how the `Driver` program with the old MapReduce API would look:

```
JobConf conf = new JobConf();
conf.setSpeculativeExecution(false);
conf.set("es.nodes", "localhost:9200");
conf.set("es.resource", "eshadoop/wordcount");
conf.setOutputFormat(EsOutputFormat.class);
conf.setMapOutputValueClass(MapWritable.class);
conf.setMapperClass(MyMapper.class);
...
JobClient.runJob(conf);
```

Going real — network monitoring data

Now that we have an idea of how to write a job that does some processing with MapReduce and pushes the data from HDFS to Elasticsearch, let's try out a real-world example to get the feel of what value we can get by performing this the ES-Hadoop way.

For illustration purposes, let's consider an example dataset of log files from a hypothetical network security and a monitoring tool. This tool acts as a gateway-cum-firewall between the devices connected in the network and the Internet. The firewall detects viruses or spyware, checks the category of the outgoing traffic, and blocks or allows the request based on the configured policies.

Getting and understanding the data

You can download the sample data generated by the tool at `https://github.com/vishalbrevitaz/eshadoop/tree/master/ch02`. Here is a snippet of the data for you to take a quick look:

```
Jan 01 12:26:26 src="10.1.1.89:0" dst="74.125.130.95"  id="None"
act="ALLOW" msg="fonts.googleapis.com/css?family=Cabin
Condensed:400,600" (sn=5QMS-CW98-F7Z5-821D, ip=192.168.1.4,
tz=Asia/Kolkata, time=Sat Jan  1 12:26:26 2000)
```

```
Dec 27 17:51:42 src="10.0.230.100:0" dst="216.163.176.37"
id="InformationTechnology" act="BLOCK"
msg="webres1.qheal.ctmail.com/SpamResolverNG/SpamResolverNG.dll?Do
NewRequest" (sn=S6RY-53CJ-MI1A-A3H1, ip=10.0.230.1,
tz=Asia/Kolkata, time=Sat Dec 27 17:51:42 2014)

Jan 01 14:05:02 src="192.168.23.7:0" dst="74.125.169.50"
id="None" act="ALLOW" msg="r13---sn-
h557snee.c.pack.google.com/crx/blobs/QwAAAHF3InbmK-
wFIemaY3I3BCN9_1dkhEVaCdgM222vuHjkxK6NBzB_0gL_ZX0viLGk2Oj9RTenoQVq
Ft4t1aRX1UBZFohm-
5P53pZvgpk0MhUAAMZSmuUMiazmP7QUhdw2GOvyfeovoIJpSQ/extension_1_4_6_
703.crx?cms_redirect=yes&expire=1419697302&ip=117.222.178.31&ipbit
s=0&mm=31&ms=au&mt=1419682885&mv=m&sparams=expire,ip,ipbits,mm,ms,
mv&signature=61E0037BE24C1E66928B6CF9410E3A8F6F845F19.0F (sn=AXN9-
Z07K-25HR-K712, ip=192.168.1.30, tz=Asia/Kolkata, time=Sat Jan  1
14:05:02 2000)

Dec 27 17:51:42 src="192.168.0.2:0" dst="23.58.43.27"
id="InformationTechnology" act="BLOCK" msg="gtssl-
ocsp.geotrust.com/" (sn=RH9P-5Y51-S4N0-M9JK, ip=192.168.0.162,
tz=Asia/Kolkata, time=Sat Dec 27 17:51:42 2014)

Dec 27 12:21:42 src="10.1.1.5:0" dst="212.56.73.9"  id="None"
act="ALLOW" msg="\220L4\001" (sn=VCNY-RD87-A6LT-IXTT, ip=, tz=,
time=Sat Dec 27 12:21:42 2014)

Dec 27 17:51:42 src="10.3.15.7:0" dst="103.243.111.210"
id="InformationTechnology" act="BLOCK"
msg="resolver1.qheal.ctmail.com/SpamResolverNG/SpamResolverNG.dll?
DoNewRequest" (sn=K6KR-U5ST-SQ7R-QV9S, ip=10.3.15.1,
tz=Asia/Kolkata, time=Sat Dec 27 17:51:42 2014)
```

We can see that the data contains a few useful pieces of information, such as the date and the source IP address, from which the request originated the destination IP address. id represents the category of the website, followed by act and msg that represents the action taken for the request, and the target URL of the request.

Knowing the problems

We have piles of logs being generated every second, and we would like to have an insight into the following aspects:

- Which are the top browsing categories?
- Which are the top domains?
- Which are the top blocked domains?
- Which are the top categories surfed by certain IP ranges?

- Which IP addresses have the most blocked requests?
- Which are the top domains for certain IP ranges?
- Who are the top targets of the attacks?
- Who are the top attackers?
- Which are the top viruses?

There can be many more such problems you may want to get answered out of these log files.

Solution approaches

Now, we have got the data and the problems that can be solved by performing some aggregations and analysis. We also know how to write MapReduce jobs with Hadoop. Most of the preceding problems are mainly centered around getting the top results for some specific fields — for example, finding the top categories, top domains, or top attackers.

At a very high level, there are two possible approaches to performing Top N queries:

- **Preaggregate the results**: This is aware of the question beforehand, writes a job to calculate Top N for a specific field of your interest, and stores the aggregated result in a file that can be queried later.
- **Aggregate the results at query-time**: This stores the granular data in a rich analytics engine (such as Elasticsearch) and asks the Top N questions on-the-fly as it comes to your mind. This performs query-time aggregation to find the Top N results.

Approach 1 – Preaggregate the results

In this approach, we need to know the question in advance. For example, which are the top 10 categories? Based on the question/s, we will write our MapReduce jobs to calculate the results that will be stored in the HDFS file.

One might think that the Top N operation can be simply combined to the logic of the reducer that we developed for the WordCount job. This may work fine if you use a single reducer. However, a single reducer would not scale well for the large datasets. This approach would not work with multiple reducers because each reducer would be working only on a subset of the data.

In order to derive the required results, we need to perform the following two steps:

1. Calculate the count of requests for each browsing category.
2. Sort the results and find the Top N categories.

To implement the use case with the MapReduce paradigm, both of these steps will need a dedicated MapReduce job. This is required because we will perform two separate aggregation operations when we calculate Top N — the count occurrences for each category — and then find the Top N categories.

First, the MapReduce job takes the raw log files as the input and produces the results that look similar to our WordCount job. For example, the job to count the categories may produce an output similar to the following code:

```
advertisements      500
informationtechnology      8028
newsandmedia    304
none    12316
portals    2945
searchengines    1323
spywaresandp2p  1175
...
...
...
```

This output can be written to the temporary file in HDFS, is provided as an input to the second MapReduce job that calculates Top N, and writes the result to the HDFS file. By performing this, you will obtain the Top N results of one field, which in this case is `category`. Great! Similarly, counter jobs have to be created for each field that you are interested in, such as attacker, IP range, blocked domains, viruses, and so on. That's not so cool!

The following diagram shows how the solution would look with this approach to obtain the answers for all the preceding Top N questions:

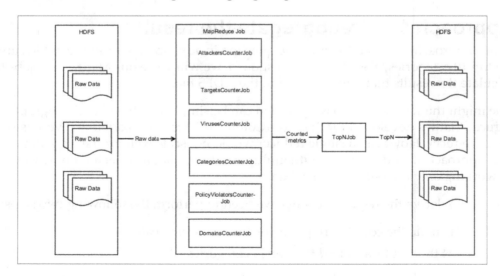

Approach 2 – Aggregate the results at query-time

The same set of questions can be answered very easily if we get the capability of performing the calculation at query-time. Elasticsearch does exactly that by providing the query-time aggregation capabilities on the indexed data. All we need to do is get the granular data indexed in Elasticsearch. Once we have done this, we can ask questions as they come to our mind, which you may not have thought of earlier. This makes our life so much easier when it comes to exploring the data.

In order to implement this approach, we will write a single MapReduce job that parses raw data from the HDFS file and uses the ES-Hadoop library to index the granular data in the Elasticsearch index.

We can leverage Elasticsearch's querying capabilities to obtain answers to our Top N questions in a fraction of a second. Elasticsearch will perform these aggregations on its distributed nodes in the cluster at runtime when we query the data. This gives us the ability to discover the data and find interesting insights from it.

The following diagram shows the solution approach with Elasticsearch to perform query-time aggregation:

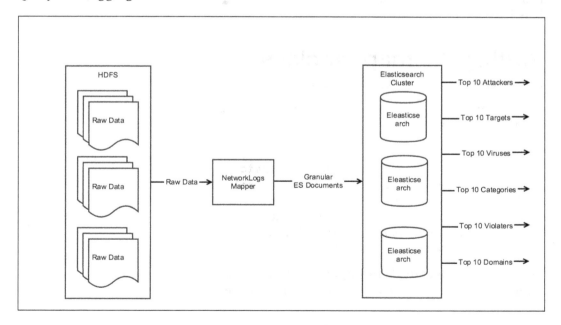

> We will gain a lot with Elasticsearch when it comes to performing discovery on data or performing exploratory analysis on data; there is a trade-off against storage and computation power. Depending on the analysis you use for your full-text search needs and the replication factor you select, you need additional storage capacity. Similarly, you need a higher amount of memory in order to compute aggregations at query-time with high performance. We will touch these topics in detail in the later part of the book.

Let's see how we can write the NetworkLogsMapper job to get the network logs data to Elasticsearch.

Writing the NetworkLogsMapper job

Now that we know the approach to getting answers to our problems elegantly, let's go ahead and write the mapper that we discussed in the previous section.

Here is the relevant part of the NetworkLogsMapper class to map our network logs to Elasticsearch.

Writing the mapper class

Let's take a look at the mapper class now:

```
public class NetworkLogsMapper extends Mapper<Object, Text, Text,
MapWritable> {

    public void map(Object key, Text value, Context context)
throws IOException, InterruptedException {
        MapWritable map = new MapWritable();
        String line = value.toString().trim();
        String[] parts = line.split(" \\(");
        String keyVals = parts[0].substring(15,
parts[0].length()).trim();
```

The preceding code reads the input log line and divides it into two easily parsable segments that contain the key/value pairs, parts and keyVals:

```
        int i = 0;
        StringTokenizer part1tokenizer = new
StringTokenizer(keyVals);
        while (part1tokenizer.hasMoreTokens()) {
            String token = part1tokenizer.nextToken();
            String keyPart = getKeyValue(token)[0];
```

```
                    String valuePart = getKeyValue(token)[1];
                    switch (keyPart) {
                        case "src":
                            srcIp = valuePart;
                            break;
                        case "dst":
                            destIp = valuePart;
                            break;
                        case "id":
                            category = valuePart;
                            break;
                        case "act":
                            action = valuePart != null ?
valuePart.toUpperCase() : null;
                            break;
                        case "msg":
                            target = valuePart;
                            break;
                    }
                    i++;
            }
```

The preceding code iterates through each of the key/value pair token of `keyVals` to extract the `sourceIp`, `destIp`, `category`, `action`, and `msg` fields.

```
            i = 0;
            if (parts.length > 1) {
                StringTokenizer part2Tokenizer = new
  StringTokenizer(parts[1], ",");
                while (part2Tokenizer.hasMoreTokens()) {
                    String token = part2Tokenizer.nextToken();
                    String keyPart = getKeyValue(token)[0];
                    String valuePart = getKeyValue(token)[1];
                    switch (keyPart) {
                        case "sn":
                            serial = valuePart;
                            break;
                        case "ip":
                            ip = valuePart;
                            break;
                        case "tz":
                            timezone = valuePart;
                            break;
                        case "time":
                            String timeStr = valuePart;
```

```
                            timeStr = timeStr.replaceAll("\\)", "");
                            SimpleDateFormat dateFormat = new
        SimpleDateFormat("EEE MMM dd hh:mm:ss YYYY");
                            try {
                                time =
        dateFormat.parse(timeStr).getTime();
                            } catch (ParseException e) {
                                e.printStackTrace();
                            }
                            break;
                    }
                    i++;
                }
```

Here is the parse `parts` segment to extract the `serial`, `ip`, `timezone`, and `time` fields:

```
        map.put(new Text("srcIp"), getWritableValue(srcIp));
        map.put(new Text("destIp"), getWritableValue(destIp));
        map.put(new Text("action"), getWritableValue(action));
        map.put(new Text("category"), getWritableValue(category));
        map.put(new Text("target"), getWritableValue(target));
        map.put(new Text("serial"), getWritableValue(serial));
        map.put(new Text("timezone"), getWritableValue(timezone));
        map.put(new Text("ip"), getWritableValue(ip));
        map.put(new
    Text("domain"),getWritableValue(getDomainName(target)));
        map.put(new Text("@timestamp"), time != null ? new
    LongWritable(time) : new LongWritable(new Date().getTime()));

        context.write(value, map);
```

Once we have parsed all the required fields from the log line, we can put all these values into the `MapWritable` object. Note that `MapWritable` needs to have all its keys and values of the `Writable` type. The preceding code gets the `Writable` versions of each field and writes them to the `MapWritable` object. Finally, the map is written in the `context` object, as shown in the following code:

```
    private static WritableComparable getWritableValue(String
value) {
        return value != null ? new Text(value) :
NullWritable.get();
    }
```

The getWritableValue() method takes the String parameter and returns a null-safe Writable value as follows:

```
public static String getDomainName(String url) {
    if(url==null)
        return null;
    return DomainUtil.getBaseDomain(url);
}
```

The getDomainName() method extracts the base domain from the URL that is provided as a parameter. The indexing domain name can help in knowing the top domains and their related analysis.

Overall, in the preceding program, we will get the input network logs in the unstructured format. We just developed a simple program that allows you to parse these log files and tries to extract the relevant information for our Elasticsearch documents.

We will also perform the required data type transformations that are expected by Elasticsearch. We parsed the timestamp from the logs from the end of the input line and converted it to the LongWritable object.

> You may have seen that we never told Elasticsearch about the fields we will index and the data type of the fields. This is handled by the automatic type mapping support provided by Elasticsearch. This automatic type mapping triggers when the first document is indexed. Elasticsearch automatically detects and creates the data types for the fields based on the value that is passed to the object.

To understand how Elasticsearch treats different data types passed from Hadoop, consider the following table as a reference:

Hadoop Class	Elasticsearch Type
NullWritable, null	This class specifies null
BooleanWritable	This class denotes Boolean
Text, MD5Writable, UTF8	This class specifies string
ByteWritable	This class denotes byte
IntWritable, VInt	This class indicates int
LongWritable, VLongWritable	This class specifies long
FloatWritable	This class denotes float
ShortWritable	This class indicates short

Hadoop Class	Elasticsearch Type
`ArrayWritable`	This class specifies array
`AbstractMapWritable`	This class denotes object
`Text` (in ISO8601 dateTime format)	This class indicates date

Writing Driver

The `Driver` class looks mostly the same as the one in the WordCount job. The `Driver` class snippet looks similar to the following code:

```
// Create configuration object for the jobConfiguration conf = new
Configuration();
// Elasticsearch Server nodes to point to
conf.set("es.nodes", "localhost:9200");
// Elasticsearch index and type name in {indexName}/{typeName}
format
conf.set("es.resource", "esh_network/network_logs_{action}");
```

We have set the `es.resource` value to `esh_network/network_logs_{action}`. This uses the dynamic or multiresource write feature provided by ES-Hadoop. This dynamically creates a new index for each new value found for the `action` field, as shown in the following code:

```
// Create Job instance with conf
Job job = new Job(conf, "network monitor mapper");
// set Driver class
job.setJarByClass(Driver.class);
job.setMapperClass(NetworkLogsMapper.class);
// set OutputFormat to EsOutputFormat provided by Elasticsearch-
Hadoop jar
job.setOutputFormatClass(EsOutputFormat.class);
job.setNumReduceTasks(0);
FileInputFormat.addInputPath(job, new Path(args[0]));

System.exit(job.waitForCompletion(true) ? 0 : 1);
```

Now, let's create the `Job` instance with the `conf` object. We no longer need to set `outputKeyClass` and `outputValueClass`. As expected, we didn't declare any reducer. Also, the number of reducer tasks must be set to `0`.

You may have use cases—such as network logs—where you get millions of logs indexed on a daily basis. In such cases, it may be desirable to have the data split into several indices. Elasticsearch supports the `SimpleDateFormat` date patterns to be provided as a template for the index name or the type name, as shown in the following code:

```
es.resource =
esh_network_{@timestamp:YYYY.MM.dd}/network_logs_{action}
```

This creates a new index whenever a new date is encountered in the document being indexed.

Building the job

In order to run the Hadoop job JAR file, we need to have the required dependent JAR files in the Hadoop classpath. We will build a fat JAR file by embedding all the required dependencies in it. For this job, these dependencies include `hadoop-core`, `hadoop-hdfs`, and `elasticsearch-hadoop`.

Here is the code snippet from the `pom.xml` file:

```xml
<dependencies>
    <dependency>
        <groupId>org.apache.hadoop</groupId>
        <artifactId>hadoop-core</artifactId>
        <version>1.2.1</version>
    </dependency>
    <dependency>
        <groupId>org.apache.hadoop</groupId>
        <artifactId>hadoop-hdfs</artifactId>
        <version>2.6.0</version>
    </dependency>
    <dependency>
        <groupId>org.elasticsearch</groupId>
        <artifactId>elasticsearch-hadoop</artifactId>
        <version>2.1.0</version>
        <exclusions>
            <exclusion>
                <artifactId>cascading-hadoop</artifactId>
                <groupId>cascading</groupId>
            </exclusion>
            <exclusion>
                <artifactId>cascading-local</artifactId>
                <groupId>cascading</groupId>
            </exclusion>
```

```
        </exclusions>
      </dependency>
  </dependencies>
```

The `<dependencies>` section declares the required `hadoop` and `elasticsearch-hadoop` dependencies, as shown in the following code:

```xml
<plugin>
    <artifactId>maven-assembly-plugin</artifactId>
    <version>2.2.1</version>

    <executions>
        <execution>
            <id>make-network-logs-job</id>
            <configuration>
                <descriptors>
                    <descriptor>assembly.xml</descriptor>
                </descriptors>
                <archive>
                    <manifest>
                        <mainClass>com.packtpub.esh.nwlogs.Driver</mainClass>
                    </manifest>
                </archive>
                <finalName>${artifactId}-${version}-nwlogs</finalName>
            </configuration>
            <phase>package</phase>
            <goals>
                <goal>single</goal>
            </goals>
        </execution>
    </executions>
</plugin>
```

The preceding code snippet shows the plugin declaration for `maven-assembly-plugin`. This plugin provides a way to customize how the JAR file is assembled. The highlighted text declares the `Driver` class as the main class for the JAR file. This assembly is explained in the configured `assembly.xml` descriptor as follows:

```xml
<assembly>
  <id>job</id>
  <formats>
    <format>jar</format>
```

```
      </formats>
      <includeBaseDirectory>false</includeBaseDirectory>
      <dependencySets>
        <dependencySet>
          <unpack>false</unpack>
          <scope>runtime</scope>
          <outputDirectory>lib</outputDirectory>
          <excludes>
            <exclude>${groupId}:${artifactId}</exclude>
          </excludes>
        </dependencySet>
        <dependencySet>
          <unpack>true</unpack>
          <includes>
            <include>${groupId}:${artifactId}</include>
          </includes>
        </dependencySet>
      </dependencySets>
    </assembly>
```

The `assembly.xml` descriptor instructs Maven that the third-party dependency JARs should be assembled in the JAR under the `lib` directory.

> Alternatively, you can also specify the JAR files to be added in the classpath by setting `HADOOP_CLASSPATH` environment variable as shown below, as shown in the following code:
>
> ```
> | HADOOP_CLASSPATH="<colon-separated-
> paths-to-custom-jars-including-elasticsearch-hadoop>"
> ```
>
> These JARs can also be made available at runtime from the command line as follows:
>
> ```
> | $ hadoop jar your-jar.jar -libjars elasticsearch-hadoop.
> jar
> ```

Once you have your `pom.xml` and `assembly.xml` configured, you are ready to build the job JAR file. Switch to the parent directory of the `pom.xml` file and execute the following command:

```
$ mvn package
```

This step assumes that you have the Maven binaries configured in the `$PATH` environment variable. This command generates the required JAR file with the `ch02-0.0.1-nwlogs-job.jar` name under the `target` folder of your project directory.

Getting the data into HDFS

Now that we have the data file and our job JAR file ready, let's import the data file to HDFS with the following commands:

```
$ hadoop fs -mkdir /input/ch02
$ hadoop fs -put data/network-logs.txt /input/ch02/network-logs.txt
```

Running the job

Let' s execute the job with the `network-logs.txt` file using the following command:

```
$ hadoop jar target/ch02-0.0.1-nwlogs-job.jar /input/ch02/network-logs.
txt
```

The ES-Hadoop metrics of the output execution looks similar to the following code (this shows that a total of 31,583 documents were sent from ES-Hadoop and accepted by Elasticsearch):

```
Elasticsearch Hadoop Counters
    Bulk Retries=0
    Bulk Retries Total Time(ms)=0
    Bulk Total=32
    Bulk Total Time(ms)=3420
    Bytes Accepted=10015094
    Bytes Received=128000
    Bytes Retried=0
    Bytes Sent=10015094
    Documents Accepted=31583
    Documents Received=0
    Documents Retried=0
    Documents Sent=31583
    Network Retries=0
    Network Total Time(ms)=3515
    Node Retries=0
    Scroll Total=0
    Scroll Total Time(ms)=0
```

The following screenshot shows the Elasticsearch Head screen with the indexed document:

We can see that the job execution generated two types in the index: `network_logs_ALLOW` and `network_logs_BLOCK`. Here, `ALLOW` and `DENY` refers to the values of the `action` field used in the multiresource naming.

Viewing the Top N results

Now that we have got our granular data indexed in Elasticsearch, let's see how we can get answers to our Top N queries.

In order to execute Elasticsearch queries, you may either use the Sense interface or the cURL command-line utility to send REST requests to Elasticsearch. If you wish to use cURL, verify that you have cURL installed by executing the following cURL command:

```
$ curl -version
```

To view the top five categories across all the network logs that we have indexed, execute the following query:

```
$ curl -XPOST http://localhost:9200/esh_network/_search?pretty -d '{
    "aggs": {
        "top-categories": {
            "terms": {
                "field": "category",
                "size": 5
            }
        }
    },
    "size": 0
}'
```

Executing the preceding command should show the following response:

```
{
  "took" : 14,
  "timed_out" : false,
..
..
  },
  "aggregations" : {
    "top-categories" : {
      "doc_count_error_upper_bound" : 26,
      "sum_other_doc_count" : 4036,
      "buckets" : [ {
        "key" : "none",
        "doc_count" : 12316
      }, {
        "key" : "informationtechnology",
        "doc_count" : 8028
      }, {
        "key" : "portals",
        "doc_count" : 2945
      }, {
        "key" : "global_wl",
        "doc_count" : 2935
      }, {
```

```
      "key" : "searchengines",
      "doc_count" : 1323
   } ]
 }
}
}
```

We can just focus on the `aggregations` part of the result as of now. You will learn about the Elasticsearch query and its response structures in detail in the next chapter.

Getting data from Elasticsearch to HDFS

So far, you learned how the ES-Hadoop library could help you in getting the data from HDFS to the Elasticsearch index. There can be use cases when you have already got your data in Elasticsearch and want to select some specific subset from this data for complex analysis. This subset can be constrained by some full-text search criteria as well.

Understanding the Twitter dataset

Twitter provides the REST API to access the Twitter data. Out of the wide range of data provided by the Twitter API, we will just focus on the tweets data with the *#elasticsearch* and *#kibana* hashtags. The dataset has been dumped in the CSV file in the following format:

```
"602491467697881088","RT @keskival: We won #IndustryHack
@CybercomFinland #Elasticsearch #Logstash #Kibana #MarkovChain
#AnomalyDetection https://t.co/Iwes6VVSqk","Sun May 24 20:38:54
IST 2015","Cybercom Finland","<a
href=""http://twitter.com/download/iphone""
rel=""nofollow"">Twitter for iPhone</a>"
"602558729087758336","RT @keskival: We won #IndustryHack
@CybercomFinland #Elasticsearch #Logstash #Kibana #MarkovChain
#AnomalyDetection https://t.co/Iwes6VVSqk","Mon May 25 01:06:10
IST 2015","Ilkka Tengvall","<a
href=""https://about.twitter.com/products/tweetdeck""
rel=""nofollow"">TweetDeck</a>"
"602588512811089920","RT @segnior_david: @doxchile, we are
implementing #RealTimeProgramming @elastic is a pretty awesome
tool, #kibana #kopf #erlang #riak http:…","Mon May 25 03:04:31 IST
2015","Leonardo Menezes","<a
href=""http://twitter.com/download/iphone""
rel=""nofollow"">Twitter for iPhone</a>"
```

```
"602799066527997952","5 Great #Reasons to #Upgrade to #Kibana 4 -
Logz.io - http://t.co/N65yWeOYEg #log","Mon May 25 17:01:11 IST
2015","Frag","<a href=""http://getfalcon.pro""
rel=""nofollow"">The Real Falcon Pro</a>"
"602821180467322880","RT @elastic: Kurrently in #Kibana: We're on
the road to 4.1 release. PAUSE for a moment to see new features
http://t.co/ZeTvtkxnBy http://t…","Mon May 25 18:29:03 IST
2015","Luiz H. Z. Santana","<a href=""http://twitter.com""
rel=""nofollow"">Twitter Web Client</a>"
"602825146878009344","Having fun playing around with geo ip
#elasticsearch #logstash #kibana","Mon May 25 18:44:49 IST
2015","Alex Gläser","<a href=""http://twitter.com""
rel=""nofollow"">Twitter Web Client</a>"
"602825343469232128","RT @APGlaeser: Having fun playing around
with geo ip #elasticsearch #logstash #kibana","Mon May 25 18:45:36
IST 2015","search-tech-bot","<a href=""https://roundteam.co""
rel=""nofollow"">RoundTeam</a>"
```

The data represents the fields, such as id, text, timestamp, user, source, and so on, in the CSV format.

Trying it yourself

Now, let's implement what you have learned so far with the Twitter dataset. Try and load the preceding Twitter dataset into Elasticsearch using the MapReduce job. This is similar to what we did for the WordCount and NetworkLogsMapper job in the last section.

The Elasticsearch document should look similar to the following code:

```
{
    "text": "RT @elastic: .@PrediktoIoT gives users realtime sensor
data analysis w/ #elasticsearch & #Spark. Here's how
http://t.co/oECqzBWZvh http://t…",
    "@timestamp": 1420246531000,
    "user": "Mario Montag",
    "tweetId": "601914318221750272"
}
```

Creating the MapReduce job to import data from Elasticsearch to HDFS

I am sure that you already have the Twitter dataset in your Elasticsearch index. If not, you can always navigate to the source code of the chapter and run the target/ch02-0.0.1-tweets2es-job.jar job to get the data into Elasticsearch.

You may want to perform complex analysis—for example, sentiment analysis of the tweets that relate to a specific criteria on the Twitter data. Let's consider that you want to do so on the data that relates to any two of the elasticsearch, kibana, analysis, visualize, and realtime terms. To be able to perform such analysis, you may want to run the MapReduce tasks on the relevant data.

Now, let's create a job that queries the data as required from Elasticsearch and imports it to HDFS.

Writing the Tweets2Hdfs mapper

Here is the Tweets2HdfsMapper class to map the MapWritable representation of Elasticsearch documents to the CSV output file to be written to HDFS:

```
public class Tweets2HdfsMapper extends Mapper<Object, MapWritable,
Text, Text> {

    public void map(Object key, MapWritable value, Context
context) throws IOException, InterruptedException {
```

When we will write a MapReduce job that reads from Elasticsearch, remember that we will get MapWritable as the input in our Mapper class. Our output will be Text that will eventually be written to a CSV file in HDFS:

```
        StringBuilder mappedValueBuilder = new StringBuilder();
        mappedValueBuilder.append(getQuotedValue(value.get(new
Text("tweetId")))+", ");
        mappedValueBuilder.append(getQuotedValue(value.get(new
Text("text")))+", ");
        mappedValueBuilder.append(getQuotedValue(value.get(new
Text("user")))+", ");
        mappedValueBuilder.append(getQuotedTimeValue(value.get(new
Text("@timestamp"))));

        Text mappedValue = new
Text(mappedValueBuilder.toString());
        context.write(mappedValue, mappedValue);
    }
```

In the preceding snippet, we will just build a String that represents a single line of the CSV file. The code appends the quoted tweetId, text, user, and timestamp fields in the CSV format. Here is an example:

```
"601078026596687873", "RT @elastic: This week in @Elastic: all
things #Elasticsearch, #Logstash, #Kibana, community & ecosystem
https://t.co/grAEffXek1", "Leslie Hawthorn", "Wed Dec 31 11:02:23
IST 2015"
```

```
    private String getQuotedTimeValue(Writable writable) {
        Date timestamp = new
Date(Long.parseLong(writable.toString()));
        SimpleDateFormat dateFormat = new SimpleDateFormat("EEE
MMM dd hh:mm:ss zzz YYYY");
        return "\""+dateFormat.format(timestamp)+"\"";
    }

    private String getQuotedValue(Writable value) {
        return "\""+value.toString()+"\"";
    }

}
```

The preceding two methods are handy to quickly get the quoted String or Date values for Writable values.

Now, let's write the Driver class, as shown in the following code:

```
public static void main(String args[]) throws IOException,
ClassNotFoundException, InterruptedException {

        // Create Configuration instance
        Configuration conf = new Configuration();
        // Elasticsearch Server nodes to point to
        conf.set("es.nodes", "localhost:9200");
        // Elasticsearch index and type name in
{indexName}/{typeName} format
        conf.set("es.resource", "esh/tweets");
        conf.set("es.query", query);
```

First, the Driver class sets the Elasticsearch node and resource to the index where the tweets are already indexed. Then, the es.query configuration specifies the query to be used when you fetch the data from the Elasticsearch index. If the es.query configuration is missing, the ES-Hadoop library queries all the documents from the index and provides them as the MapWritable input to the Mapper class, as shown in the following code:

```
        // Create Job instance
        Job job = new Job(conf, "tweets to hdfs mapper");
        // set Driver class
        job.setJarByClass(Driver.class);
        job.setMapperClass(Tweets2HdfsMapper.class);
        // set IntputFormat to EsInputFormat provided by
Elasticsearch-Hadoop jar
```

```
job.setInputFormatClass(EsInputFormat.class);
job.setNumReduceTasks(0);
FileOutputFormat.setOutputPath(job, new Path(args[0]));

System.exit(job.waitForCompletion(true) ? 0 : 1);
}
```

The important configuration to note here is `setInputFormatClass(EsInputForm at.class)`. This tells Hadoop to read the input from Elasticsearch. The ES-Hadoop library reads the documents as mentioned by the `es.query` configuration and provides as the `MapWritable` input to the `mapper` class.

In the preceding example, the `query` variable refers to the following Elasticsearch query in the JSON format (we will get a detailed understanding of such queries in the next chapter):

```
{
  "query": {
    "bool": {
      "should": [
        {
          "term": {
            "text": {
              "value": "elasticsearch"
            }


          }
        },{
          "term": {
            "text": {
              "value": "kibana"
            }


          }
        },{
          "term": {
            "text": {
              "value": "analysis"
            }


          }
        },{
          "term": {
            "text": {
              "value": "visualize"
```

```
              }

            }
        },{
          "term": {
            "text": {
              "value": "realtime"
            }

          }
        }
      ],
      "minimum_number_should_match": 2
    }

  }
}
```

The `es.query` configuration can be in one of the following three formats:

- As a URI or a parameter query, as shown in the following code:

  ```
  es.query = "?q=Elasticsearch"
  ```

- Query DSL in the JSON format, as used in the `Twitter2Hdfs` example

  ```
  es.query = { "query" : { "term" : { "text" :
  "elasticsearch" } } }
  ```

- External resource path

  ```
  es.query = org/queries/Elasticsearch-tweets-query.json
  ```

> If the URI and the QueryDSL formats are not found for `es.query`, ES-Hadoop tries to find the resource in the HDFS, classpath, or the Hadoop-distributed cache respectively with the same name. The file must contain the query in the URI or the QueryDSL format.

Running the example

Once you have built the JAR file with dependencies, you can run the job to load the data from Elasticsearch to HDFS.

Now, execute the following command to run the example:

```
$ hadoop jar <LOCATION_OF_JOB_JAR_FILE>/ch02-0.0.1-tweets2hdfs-job.jar /
output/ch02/
```

 Make sure that the output directory mentioned as a command-line argument must not already exist in the HDFS. This will happen if you try to run the same job twice or more. In such a case, you can either change the output directory or delete it with the hadoop `fs -rm -r /output/ch02/` command.

This command execution should display the output for the provided Twitter sample data, as shown in the following code:

```
Elasticsearch Hadoop Counters
Bulk Retries=0
Bulk Retries Total Time(ms)=0
Bulk Total=0
Bulk Total Time(ms)=0
Bytes Accepted=0
Bytes Received=138731
Bytes Retried=0
Bytes Sent=4460
Documents Accepted=0
Documents Received=443
Documents Retried=0
Documents Sent=0
Network Retries=0
Network Total Time(ms)=847
Node Retries=0
Scroll Total=10
Scroll Total Time(ms)=195
```

The console output for the execution shows that the number of documents received from Elasticsearch is 443.

Testing the job execution output

First, let's check whether the job successfully generated the CSV file for the expected tweet data. To verify that the output files are generated successfully, execute the following command:

```
$ hadoop fs -ls /output/ch02/
```

Now, the successful execution of the command should print the console output, as shown in the following code:

```
Found 6 items
-rw-r--r--   1 eshadoop supergroup          0 2015-05-27 23:08 /output/
ch02/_SUCCESS
-rw-r--r--   1 eshadoop supergroup      36494 2015-05-27 23:08 /output/
ch02/part-m-00000
-rw-r--r--   1 eshadoop supergroup      36684 2015-05-27 23:08 /output/
ch02/part-m-00001
-rw-r--r--   1 eshadoop supergroup      38326 2015-05-27 23:08 /output/
ch02/part-m-00002
-rw-r--r--   1 eshadoop supergroup      34090 2015-05-27 23:08 /output/
ch02/part-m-00003
-rw-r--r--   1 eshadoop supergroup      32958 2015-05-27 23:08 /output/
ch02/part-m-00004
```

The job generates as many number of output files as the mapper instances. This is because we didn't have any reducer for the job.

To verify the content of the file, execute the following command:

```
$ hadoop fs -tail /output/ch02/part-m-00000
```

Now, verify that the output is similar to the one shown in the following code:

```
"914318221750272", "RT @elastic: .@PrediktoIoT gives users realtime
sensor data analysis w/ #elasticsearch & #Spark. Here's how http://t.co/
oECqzBWZvh http://t…", "Mario Montag", "Sat Jan 03 06:25:31 IST 2015"
"601914318221750272", "RT @elastic: .@PrediktoIoT gives users realtime
sensor data analysis w/ #elasticsearch & #Spark. Here's how http://t.co/
oECqzBWZvh http://t…", "Mario Montag", "Sat Jan 03 06:25:31 IST 2015"

"602223267194208256", "Centralized System and #Docker Logging with
#ELK Stack #elasticsearch #logstash #kibana  http://t.co/MIn7I52Okl",
"Joël Vimenet", "Sun Dec 28 02:53:10 IST 2015"   "602223267194208256",
"Centralized System and #Docker Logging with #ELK Stack #elasticsearch
#logstash #kibana  http://t.co/MIn7I52Okl", "Joël Vimenet", "Sun Dec 28
02:53:10 IST 2015"

"603461899456483328", "#Elasticsearch using in near realtime", "Ilica
Brnadi", "Wed Dec 31 12:55:03 IST 2015" "603461899456483328",
"#Elasticsearch using in near realtime", "Ilica Brnadi", "Wed Dec 31
12:55:03 IST 2015"
```

Summary

In this chapter, we discussed the `MapReduce` programs by going through the `WordCount` program. We checked how to develop the MapReduce jobs with the new and old map-reduce APIs. We delved into the details of a real-world network logs monitoring problem. You learned how to solve the problem in a better way by using the aggregation capabilities of Elasticsearch.

Further, you learned how to write and build the Hadoop MapReduce job that leverages ES-Hadoop to get the network logs monitoring data to Elasticsearch. Finally, we explored how to get the data out from Elasticsearch in the MapReduce job for the Twitter dataset. Overall, we got a complete understanding of how to get the data in and out between Elasticsearch and Hadoop.

In the next chapter, we will be dive deeper into Elasticsearch to understand Elasticsearch mappings, how the indexing process works, and how to query the Elasticsearch data in order to perform full-text search and aggregations.

3

Understanding Elasticsearch

In order to fully leverage all the analytic capabilities of Elasticsearch, Hadoop, and the Kibana stack, it is more than helpful to have a sound understanding of the basics of Elasticsearch and its querying concepts. This chapter will help you get more familiar with Elasticsearch, enable you to work with mappings, and write a full-text search and aggregation queries to get an insight from your indexed data.

In this chapter, we will cover the following topics:

- Knowing search and Elasticsearch
- Talking to Elasticsearch
- Controlling the indexing process
- Elastic searching
- Performing aggregations

Knowing Search and Elasticsearch

Search is something that can be as simple as performing an exact match on some field or finding a substring out of your document. On the other hand, it can be much more complex with the needs of knowing the matches that are more relevant to others. These matches can be performed on a humongous number of documents.

Searches can be of different types:

- **Unstructured search**: This finds candidates with experience in search technologies
- **Structured search**: This finds candidates with five to ten years of experience
- **Geo Spatial search**: This finds candidates within the radius of 200 kilometers from Mumbai

- **Analytics**: This finds the average salary of all the candidates
- **Combined**: This finds the average salary of candidates with five to ten years of experience in search technologies within the radius of 200 kilometers from Mumbai

If the amount of data you deal with is limited, fulfilling many of the preceding search needs is not so complex with relational databases. However, if your search needs unstructured data, a better performing and scalable approach could be a full-fledged, scalable search engine.

For many years, Apache Lucene had been the default choice for implementing complex text searches on structured and unstructured data. Lucene is the de facto library for implementing search and indexing. It is a feature-rich and low-level library. However, it is *very complex* to use it directly. Thus, it is difficult for application developers to leverage its value without getting into too much of low-level details.

Elasticsearch is a document-oriented search engine (built around Lucene) designed for scalability and performance. It provides high-level abstraction around Lucene to make all the types of search (including a full-text search) and analytics easier. Apart from being a search engine, Elasticsearch is a distributed, scalable, and multi-tenant document store. It is schema-free, but it allows you to have full control on the schema whenever required. It provides a RESTful interface with JSON support and a rich client API for various programming languages, such as Java, .NET, Groovy, PHP, Perl, Python, Ruby, and JavaScript.

The paradigm mismatch

Moving to Elasticsearch from a relational database background needs a paradigm shift. To get started quickly with Elasticsearch, it is helpful to understand some of the basic terminology and structure of the index. If you are familiar with relational databases, it may be useful to find some analogy on how to map the constructs of RDBMS to Elasticsearch.

Let's see how the Elasticsearch index is structured and how it maps to relational databases.

Index

Index is a collection of different types of document categorized under one logical namespace. The Elasticsearch index can be thought of as a schema in a relational database. Index is a unit where you can apply your scalability and availability settings by configuring a number of shards and replica. You don't really need to worry about shards and replica as of now to understand further concepts; we will go into the details later in the book.

Unlike relational databases, Elasticsearch indexes are multitenant. You can dynamically create and drop Elasticsearch indexes.

Type

Elasticsearch **Type** is a logical collection of documents representing the same entity. Type can be thought of as a database table. This belongs to an index and can contain documents with the *same* fields and schema. Type usually represents your domain objects, such as a tweet, an employee, a student, a company, a user, and so on. Schema can be imposed in a document at the type level. The documents in one type are logically similar and represent the same entity type.

When I said that Elasticsearch Type contains documents with the same fields, the number of fields may vary from document to document. Elasticsearch is schema-free, but it is not practical in most situations of production systems to have fully schema-less documents. Your application will need to assume some sort of fields and data types for document fields.

Document

The Elasticsearch **document** is a logical unit that represents the instance of an entity. In other words, it represents a row in relational databases. It correlates with different terms used in different languages, such as Object, Hash, HashMap, Dictionary, and so on. You can represent most objects in the form of a JSON object, where the object properties map to the respective JSON fields.

The Elasticsearch document is a JSON object that embeds the domain object in the form of JSON with additional Elasticsearch-specific metadata. We will take a look at the exact structure and its metadata in the next section.

Field

The Elasticsearch document consists of multiple fields that are organized as JSON key/value pairs. These fields can be of core data types, object types, or an array type. As the type represents a table and the document represents a row, the fields can be thought of as columns, and the field values would represent the cell value of relational database tables.

Talking to Elasticsearch

Elasticsearch is designed to make a developer's job simple when it comes to search and analytics. It is as simple as entering a single command to get started with Elasticsearch and indexing your first document with absolutely zero configuration.

CRUD with Elasticsearch

Elasticsearch provides a REST API to perform `create`, `update`, `retrieve`, and `delete` operations. Let's take a look at how to perform the basic CRUD operations with Elasticsearch.

To execute the queries, you can either use the cURL utility or the Sense interface. If you wish to use cURL, verify that you have cURL installed by executing the following cURL command:

```
$ curl -version
```

It should display the following output:

```
curl 7.35.0 (x86_64-pc-linux-gnu) libcurl/7.35.0 OpenSSL/1.0.1f
zlib/1.2.8 libidn/1.28 librtmp/2.3
```

```
Protocols: dict file ftp ftps gopher http https imap imaps ldap ldaps
pop3 pop3s rtmp rtsp smtp smtps telnet tftp
```

```
Features: AsynchDNS GSS-Negotiate IDN IPv6 Largefile NTLM NTLM_WB SSL
libz TLS-SRP
```

With cURL installed, you are all set to talk to Elasticsearch.

Creating the document request

Let's start by indexing a new Elasticsearch document with the following command:

```
$ curl -XPUT http://localhost:9200/hrms/candidate/1?pretty -d '{
  "firstName": "Emerson",
  "lastName": "Atkins",
  "skills": ["Java", "Hadoop", "Elasticsearch"]
}'
```

This command sends an HTTP PUT request to Elasticsearch using the following URL format: `http://<ES_HOST>:<PORT>/<INDEX_NAME>/<TYPE_NAME>/<UNIQUE_DOC_ID>`.

The successful execution of the preceding command should return the following response:

```
{
  "_index":"hrms",
  "_type":"candidate",
  "_id":"1",
  "_version":1,
  "created":true
}
```

The _index, _type, _id, and _version fields are the metadata of Elasticsearch that are added to the document. The created field provides an acknowledgement of whether a new document was created or not.

 We didn't have to create an index with the hrms name first. We didn't create the candidate type either.

The GET request

To retrieve the Elasticsearch document that we just indexed, execute the following command:

```
$ curl -XGET  http://localhost:9200/hrms/candidate/1?pretty
```

Now, you should see the following response:

```
{"_index":"hrms","_type":"candidate","_id":"1","_
  version":1,"found":true,"_source":{
  "firstName": "Emerson",
  "lastName": "Atkins",
  "skills": ["Java","Hadoop","Elasticsearch"]
}}
```

The response includes all the Elasticsearch document metadata, along with the original document content as the _source field.

The Update request

To update an Elasticsearch document, you can send exactly the same request as we sent to create a document. Elasticsearch will simply overwrite the old document with the new document. The documents of Elasticsearch are internally immutable, so you can just mimic the update process using *get-modify-update*. Every time you update the document, the _version metadata field is incremented by 1.

Elasticsearch also supports partial updates of the document. For example, you can add a new field experience to the document, as shown in the following command:

```
$ curl -XPOST http://localhost:9200/hrms/candidate/1/_update?pretty -d '{
  "doc":{
     "experience": 8
  }
}'
```

Now, additional fields must be provided in the doc field of the root JSON object of the request. However, remember that the Elasticsearch document is always immutable, so you can't update it. The partial update request is just a syntactic sugar. Essentially, Elasticsearch internally performs the same *get-modify-update* operation.

The Delete request

You can delete an Elasticsearch document by sending an HTTP DELETE request for the document, as shown in the following command:

```
$ curl -XDELETE  http://localhost:9200/hrms/candidate/1?pretty
```

Creating the index

If you just want to create a plain index, you can send an HTTP PUT request on endpoint with just an index name in it, as shown in the following command:

```
$ curl -XPUT http://localhost:9200/hrms?pretty
```

However, sending the preceding request throws the following error because the index already exists:

```
{
   "error": "IndexAlreadyExistsException[[hrms] already exists]",
   "status": 400
}
```

Mappings

In the previous section, we indexed a new Elasticsearch document. Note that, we did not define any mappings before indexing the document and were still able to successfully index it.

Let's check what happened with the *type mapping* of candidate by executing the following command:

```
$ curl -XGET http://localhost:9200/hrms/candidate/_mapping?pretty
```

This will return the mapping, as follows:

```
{
    "hrms": {
        "mappings": {
            "candidate": {
                "properties": {
"experience": {
                        "type": "long"
                    },
                    "firstName": {
                        "type": "string"
                    },
                    "lastName": {
                        "type": "string"
                    },
                    "skills": {
                        "type": "string"
                    }
                }
            }
        }
    }
}
```

You can see that Elasticsearch has automatically generated the mapping for the fields we provided in the document. Whenever we index a document with a new `type` or a new `field`, Elasticsearch infers the data type of the field from the field value on the best-guess basis.

It may not always be desirable to have an autogenerated mapping for *type mappings*. For example, you may want to have the `experience` field in the preceding mapping to be `float` instead of `long`. In such cases, you should have a way to define the type mapping in advance for Elasticsearch types. Apart from specifying the data types, custom mappings are essential when you wish to apply nondefault analyzers, or you want to fine-tune the field-specific index configurations. We will look at the analyzers in the next section.

Before we move on to how to create the data type mapping for your types, let's take a look at the data types supported by Elasticsearch.

Data types

Elasticsearch supports most of the core data types that we already know as well as the following core types:

- `string`
- `byte`, `short`, `int`, and `long`
- `float` and `double`
- `boolean`
- `date`

> Whenever Elasticsearch tries to infer the data type of a field, it takes the largest possible value type for the supported type. This means that if the field value is found to be 8, it will assume the data type to be `long`, whereas for 8.1, it will infer to `double`.

Apart from the preceding core types, Elasticsearch supports embedding other objects (in the form of JSON) as a part of the document. It also supports arrays, nested loops, IPv4, geo points, and geo shape types. It is beyond the scope of this book to dig into details of all these types; however, we will see examples of some of these mapping types as we go further into the book.

> Elasticsearch supports array types out of the box. This means that you don't specifically need to declare the type to be an *array* when you create the mapping. You can just pass an array value of the respective field type in the document. In the *skills* mapping in our candidate index mapping, we declared *skills* as the `string` type and passed *array of strings* as its value.

Create mapping API

You can create a new mapping for an existing index, append, or change the mapping with the PUT mapping call, as shown in the following code:

```
$ curl -XPUT http://localhost:9200/hrms/candidate/_mapping?pretty -d '{
  "properties": {
    "experience": {
      "type": "float"
    },
    "firstName": {
```

```
      "type": "string"
    },
    "lastName": {
      "type": "string"
    },
    "birthDate": {
      "type": "date",
      "format": "dd/MM/YYYY"
    },
    "salary": {
      "type": "double"
    },
    "skills": {
      "type": "string"
    },
    "address": {
      "type": "object",
      "properties": {
        "street": {
          "type": "string"
        },
        "city": {
          "type": "string",
          "index": "not_analyzed"
        },
        "region": {
          "type": "string"
        },
        "geo": {
          "type": "geo_point"
        }
      }
    }
  }
}'
```

The preceding mapping creates the mapping for candidate. This mapping shows an example mapping of date, object, and geo_point. You can use "index":"not_analyzed" to disable the analysis for the field. Elasticsearch will simply use the as-is input value as a *term* in the inverted index.

 When you dynamically update the Elasticsearch mapping, the new mapping must be compatible with the already-indexed data.

Index templates

This can be very handy when you are dealing with multitenancy. You may wish to create a new index per client, per user, or per quarter (typically termed as a rolling index). In such cases, you will have the same *type mappings* for all your indexes.

With index templates, you can define an index name pattern and provide index configurations with *type mappings* that will be automatically applied when the new index with a matching name is created, as shown in the following command:

```
$ curl -XPUT http://localhost:9200/_template/hrms-template?pretty
 -d '{
  "template": "hrms*",
  "mappings": {
    "candidate": {
      "experience": {
        "type": "float"
      }

    }
  }
}'
```

Controlling the indexing process

Fundamentally, indexing is the process that helps you search faster. The most basic example you can see of indexing is the index of a book or document. You can quickly find the topic you are looking for, the associated page number, and thus the content you are looking for.

Let's consider an example of a simple index for the following two sentences:

- Elasticsearch is an awesome search engine for fast full-text search and analytics

- Elasticsearch can help you analyze big volume data quickly

One would create an index by simply giving an `ID` to both of these sentences and splitting them into tokens, as shown in the following table:

Id	Words
1	ElasticSearch, is, an, awesome, search, engine, for, fast, full-text, and, analytics
2	ElasticSearch, can, help, you, analyze, high-volume? data, quickly

This works great if you want to find the words that exist in the given document, meaning when you have got an `ID` in hand and are looking for the information associated with the ID.

In full-text search and analytics, what you typically need is exactly the inverse, for example, which documents matches the `fast` and `search` terms? Which are the most relevant documents for the `search` word?

What is an inverted index?

An inverted index is the same as the simple index we saw, but in the reverse direction. Instead of mapping the words that belong to a particular `ID`, we would create buckets with words known as *terms* and map the `IDs` that contain that word.

Here is the vanilla version of our inverted index:

Term	Doc ID
ElasticSearch	1,2
is	1
an	1
awesome	1
search	1
engine	1
for	1
fast	1
full-text	1

Term	Doc ID
and	1
analytics	1
can	2
help	2
you	2
analyze	2
big	2
volume	2
data	2
quickly	2

The preceding index just maps the document ID to the term found in the sentences. Is there any improvement you can think of in the preceding index to make it leaner and more effective?

The input data analysis

What goes into your index affects your search results and your ability to search a particular document. Here are some of the example optimizations you can perform in your inverted index.

Removing stop words

You may want to drop the stop words, such as is, an, and, and so on, from the index, because they don't add any value when you search. The stop words are highlighted in *italics* in the preceding table.

Case insensitive

You may wish to be able to match a document that contains the Elasticsearch term when a user searches for elasticsearch. You can do so by lowercasing the input when you index it and turn the index to become case insensitive.

Stemming

Analyze and analytics essentially refer to the same thing. These can be resolved to the analysis term at the time of indexing.

Synonyms

It may be good to have `fast` and `quickly` mean the same. When you index, you can use the common term, `fast`, to index all the synonyms for it.

After applying this analysis, our inverted index would look similar to the following table:

Term	Doc ID
elasticsearch	1,2
awesome	1
search	1
engine	1
fast	1,2
full-text	1
analyze	1,2
big	1
volume	1
data	1

Lucene, and hence Elasticsearch, provides you full control over how to index your data. Elasticsearch supports analyzers to control the indexing process. Let's explore how the analysis in the preceding table can be achieved in Elasticsearch.

Analyzers

Elasticsearch allows you to specify the analyzer for a field in the *type mapping*. Analyzers are applied to the input text when you index new data. They process the input text and produces the terms to be indexed. Elasticsearch applies the same analyzers on the search term as well when you match the input text.

The following image shows how analyzers work during the indexing and querying operations:

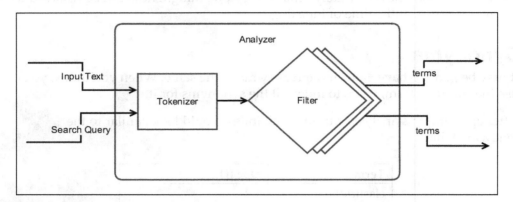

You can choose to configure analyzers at the index and search time. It is important to understand the implication of both these approaches. Although the index-time analyzer may increase your storage needs, depending on the analyzer, applying the analyzer at the query-time will affect the performance because there is more work to do during the query-time.

As shown in the preceding diagram, the **Analyzer** has a **Tokenizer** and multiple filters. Tokenizer is responsible for splitting the input text into tokens. Some of the prebuilt tokenizers that Elasticsearch ships with are whitespace, keyword, lowercase, standard, and n-gram. These tokens are then passed on to the chain of filters. The filters can modify, remove, or add new tokens. Filters are processed in the sequence that is specified in the analyzer definition. Some of the predefined token filters are lowercase, n-gram, stop token, snowball, and so on.

Elasticsearch provides a few very useful analyzers, such as standard, simple, whitespace, stop, keyword, snowball, and so on, that you can choose from.

Here is an example of how you can choose the simple analyzer for the skills field (the simple analyzer is a built-in analyzer that just applies the lowercase tokenizer):

```
{
  "properties": {
    "skills": {
      "type": "string",
      "analyzer": "simple"
    }
  }
}
```

You can create your custom analyzer when you create the index with the following command:

```
$ curl -XPUT http://localhost:9200/hrms?pretty -d '{
  "settings": {
    "analysis": {
      "analyzer": {
        "tweets_analyzer": {
          "tokenizer": "whitespace",
          "filter": ["stop", "lowercase", "snowball"]
        }
      }
    }
  }
}'
```

In the preceding example, we used the `whitespace` tokenizer to create tokens for the text separated by whitespaces. The `stop`, `lowercase`, and `snowball` filters are chained together. The `stop` filter removes the standard English stop words (as mentioned earlier), whereas the `lowercase` filter converts all the tokens to lowercase (as the name suggests). The `snowball` filter is an algorithmic stemming filter that tries to reduce the word to its root English form. It is better in terms of memory usage and works out of the box. Also, it may not work best for nonstandard words; for example, the analysis and analyze tokens would produce different terms that are not intended.

Elastic searching

Now that you know the basics of indexing, how to use the built-in and custom analyzers, how to create mapping, and index new documents, let's see how to query your indexed documents in Elasticsearch.

Writing search queries

Elasticsearch supports various query types with its Query DSL by posting a JSON-based query in the POST request body.

It is beyond the scope of this book to discuss the minute details of each query type and its configurable options. I would highly recommend that you try these queries out with different options and data to understand the query behaviors better. You can use the small dataset script provided at https://raw.githubusercontent.com/vishalbrevitaz/eshadoop/master/ch03/data/setup-hrms.sh to try out the queries mentioned in the following sections.

The URI search

Elasticsearch provides a quick way to search with the GET request by passing a criteria as the query string parameter.

Here is an example to find candidates with the elasticsearch skill:

```
$ curl -XGET http://localhost:9200/hrms/candidate/_search?pretty=true&q=s
kills:elasticsearch
```

Matching all queries

The match_all query is the simplest of all the Elasticsearch queries. It matches all the documents. Take a look at the following command:

```
$ curl -XPOST http://localhost:9200/hrms/candidate/_search?pretty -d '{
  "query":{
  "match_all": {}
  }
}'
```

The term query

The term query searches the inverted index to find the documents that exactly match the search term.

Here is the query to find all the candidates with the elasticsearch skill:

```
$ curl -XPOST http://localhost:9200/hrms/candidate/_search?pretty -d '{
  "query": {
    "term": {
      "skills": {
        "value": "elasticsearch"
      }
    }
  },
"size": 10
}'
```

When you execute this query, it returns the following result:

```
{
    "took": 1,
    "timed_out": false,
```

```json
    "_shards": {
        "total": 5,
        "successful": 5,
        "failed": 0
    },
    "hits": {
        "total": 5,
        "max_score": 2.098612,
        "hits": [
            {
                "_index": "hrms",
                "_type": "candidate",
                "_id": "AU3s4GrOdeMVyAuwkp0R",
                "_score": 2.098612,
                "_source": {
                    "firstName": "Jorden",
                    "lastName": "Mclean",
                    "birthDate": "11/03/1980",
                    "experience": 19,
                    "skills": [
                        "Java",
                        "Hadoop",
                        "Elasticsearch",
                        "Kibana"
                    ],
                    "address": {
                        "street": "2751 Ut Rd.",
                        "city": "Purral",
                        "region": "SJ",
                        "geo": "-80.61395, 21.93988"
                    },
                    "comments": "Passionate Java and BigData developer"
                }
            },
            ..
            ..
        ]
    }
}
```

Most part of the preceding result is self-explanatory. The result shows the time it took to execute the request; hits contains the total number of matching documents found, along with the list of matching documents based on the size parameter specified in the query.

> We passed the elasticsearch search term in lowercase to ensure that we get the *exact* match with the analyzed value in the inverted index. As we are explicitly trying to match the term for the term query, tokenizer and filters will not be applied to the search term.

Similarly, you can use the terms query to match any of the values out of the specified array of search terms.

The boolean query

The boolean query allows you to mimic the AND and OR operations. You can build the boolean query with multiple clauses using the MUST, MUST_NOT, and SHOULD operators. Clauses refer to any of the other types of the Elasticsearch query. MUST and MUST_NOT simply filters the results that match or don't match the respective clauses. By default, the SHOULD clause checks whether or not at least one of the clauses turns out to be true for the document.

For example, the following query finds all the candidates from Mumbai with the Elasticsearch or Lucene experience:

```
$ curl -XPOST http://localhost:9200/hrms/candidate/_search?pretty -d '{
  "query":{
    "bool": {
      "must": [
        {
          "term": {
            "address.city": {
              "value": "Mumbai"
            }
          }
        }
      ],
      "should":[
        {
          "terms": {
```

```
        "skills": ["elasticsearch",
"lucene"]
    }
        }
        ]
    }
  }
}'
```

 You can set the `minimum_number_should_match` parameter to control the number of clauses that must be matched for the document.

The match query

This comes with multiple choices that serve as a one-stop shop for your basic search needs. It allows you to query for the `text`, `numeric`, and `date` data types and enables you to control the analysis of the query as well.

The following query finds all the candidates with comments related to `hacking` or `java`:

```
$ curl -XPOST http://localhost:9200/hrms/candidate/_search?pretty  -d '{
  "query":{
    "match" : {
        "comments" : {
            "query" : "hacking java"
        }
    }
  }
}'
```

By default, the `match` query is of the `Boolean` type with the `or` operator, that is, at least one of the *hacking* or *java* should match at least one term in the `comments` field. It allows you to specify the `fuzziness` parameter as well to set the extent to which the term may tolerate misspelling.

The `match` query can also be used as the `match_phrase` query, as shown in the following command:

```
$ curl -XPOST http://localhost:9200/hrms/candidate/_search?pretty -d '{
  "query": {
    "match" : {
        "comments" : {
            "query" : "ethical hacking",
            "type" : "phrase"
        }
    }
  }
}'
```

The preceding query matches the phrase with the exact sequence in the `comments` field. You can set the `slop` parameter to define the amount of deviation in the order.

Similarly, you can set `type` to `phrase_prefix` to have the `match_phrase_prefix` behavior.

The range query

This matches the documents with the field value in the specified range. We can define ranges using the `gt`, `gte`, `lt`, and `lte` operators. These operators represent the *greater than*, *greater than or equal*, *less than*, and *less than or equal* operators respectively.

Here is the query for finding all the candidates with of 5 to 10 years of experience:

```
$ curl -XPOST http://localhost:9200/hrms/candidate/_search?pretty -d '{
  "query":{
    "range": {
      "experience": {
        "gte": 5,
        "lte": 10
      }
    }
  }
}'
```

The wildcard query

This allows `wildcard` expressions to be used in the `not_analyzed` field. You can use the `*` wildcard character to match all the characters with numerous repetitions. The `?` wildcard character works similar to `*`, but it matches only a single character.

The following query finds all the candidates from the city starting with mu:

```
$ curl -XPOST http://localhost:9200/hrms/candidate/_search?pretty -d '{
  "query": {
    "wildcard": {
      "address.city": {
        "value": "mu*"
      }
    }
  }
}'
```

 The ? and * wildcard characters should not be used in the beginning of the query string to prevent extremely slow queries.

Apart from the preceding queries, Elasticsearch supports a wide range of queries for various use cases, such as prefix query, fuzzy like this query, more like this query, common terms query, span term query, span near term query, geo shape query, and so on.

Filters

Elasticsearch queries are meant to perform relevant searches. Given a set of documents and a search query, you are not only interested in knowing whether it is a match or not, but also how closely the document matches the query. Elasticsearch performs this using the Lucene scoring method. We will not discuss the details of scoring because it is beyond the scope of the book.

Filters are similar to queries, except for the fact that filters don't deal with scoring at all. The result of a filter just returns the documents that match with the query; there is no relevant aspect to it.

 Due to the fact that filters don't need to work with relevance, they are an attractive candidate for caching purposes. If you want to just subset the documents matching a certain condition regardless of the score and have a filter matching your needs, always prefer *filters* over *queries* to get better search performance.

Let's take a look at a couple of filters that are not available as query.

The exists filter

This allows you to check the existence of the non-null value in the field. It filters out all the documents that doesn't have this field at all or has the null value.

Here is how you can find all the candidates with the achievements field as not null:

```
$ curl -XPOST http://localhost:9200/hrms/candidate/_search?pretty -d '{
  "query": {
    "filtered": {
      "filter": {
        "exists":{
          "field":"achievements"
        }
      }
    }
  }
}'
```

The geo distance filter

This allows you to match the locations mapped as the geo_point type within a specified radius.

Here is how you can find all the candidates within 50 kilometers of the reference geo point:

```
$ curl -XPOST http://localhost:9200/hrms/candidate/_search?pretty -d '{
  "query":{
    "filtered" : {
      "query" : {
        "match_all" : {}
      },
      "filter" : {
        "geo_distance": {
          "distance": "80km",
          "address.geo" : {
            "lat" : 23.05,
            "lon" : 72.97
          }
```

```
            }
         }
      }
   }
}'
```

Elasticsearch supports the `and`, `or`, `bool`, `ids`, `geo polygon`, `geo distance`, and `range` filters that can be helpful to fulfill your specific needs or to use as an alternative to the respective query.

Aggregations

Elasticsearch provides an aggregation module to retrieve the analytic information on the huge dataset indexed in Elasticsearch. Aggregations are similar to what we knew as the GROUP BY clause and aggregate functions in the relational database world. You can execute aggregations on a subset of the overall indexed data by restricting the dataset using any Elasticsearch query that you learned in the last section. Each cluster node locally executes aggregations. The result collected by each node is then aggregated to derive the final aggregation result.

Aggregations can be categorized into two broad types:

- **Bucketing:** This type of aggregation can be seen as the enriched GROUP BY clause of SQL. It categorizes documents into buckets based on a specific criterion.

- **Metrics**: These are similar to the aggregate functions of SQL. They perform computations, such as `simple count`, `average`, `sum`, `percentile`, and so on, on a specified field of the document set.

> Elasticsearch provides real-time results. This runs on top of the big amount of data and needs you to trade it with exactness. The results of Elasticsearch aggregation are accurate, but not 100 percent exact. In practical situations, this is not an issue with most of the domains. The 0.5 percent error of the approximate results is hardly an issue, especially when you are dealing with Big Data in real time.

Executing the aggregation queries

Let's take a look at some of the widely-used aggregations in action.

The terms aggregation

This works on the terms indexed for a specific field. You can set the size to find the Top N results for a certain field.

Here is how you can find the top three cities from where all the candidates are from:

```
$ curl -XPOST http://localhost:9200/hrms/candidate/_search?pretty -d '{
  "aggs": {
    "candidates_by_region": {
      "terms": {
        "field": "address.city",
        "size": 3
      }
    }
  }
}'
```

Executing this query should return a result similar to the one shown in the following code:

```
{
    "took": 2,
    "timed_out": false,
    "_shards": {
        "total": 5,
        "successful": 5,
        "failed": 0
    },
    "hits": {
        "total": 13,
        "max_score": 1,
        "hits": [
            {
            ...
        ...
            }
  ] ,
        "aggregations": {
            "candidates_by_region": {
            "doc_count_error_upper_bound": 0,
```

```
        "sum_other_doc_count": 3,
        "buckets": [
          {
              "key": "Akron",
              "doc_count": 2
          },
          {
              "key": "New South Wales",
              "doc_count": 2
          },
          {
              "key": "Parramatta",
              "doc_count": 2
          }
        ]
      }
    }
  }
}
```

You can find the bottom N results by specifying the ascending order for count, as shown in the following code:

```
"terms": {
        "field": "address.city",
        "size": 3,

        "order": {
          "_count": "asc"
        }
}
```

The result of the aggregation query returns hits matched with the query as well as the aggregations. This is highlighted in the result. The aggregation result contains key for each bucket (along with doc_count) that matches the query criteria for the term. You may be interested in just having the aggregation results. You can achieve this by setting the size parameter of the request to 0.

You must set the field indexing to not_analyzed when you intend to use the field for the terms aggregation to avoid tons of unwanted tokens in the aggregation results.

Histograms

To build the histogram chart over the numeric field using consistent intervals, Elasticsearch provides the histogram aggregation.

The following query provides the document counts with buckets of 3 years experience ranges:

```
$ curl -XPOST http://localhost:9200/hrms/candidate/_search?pretty -d '{
  "aggs": {
    "cand_exp_dist": {
      "histogram": {
        "field": "experience",
        "interval": 3,
        "min_doc_count": 0
      }
    }
  }
}'
```

The range aggregation

You may want to build a histogram chart with a consistent interval range. You can achieve this using the range aggregation. This allows you to specify the exact ranges of the numeric data type or the date data type in order to create buckets.

Here is how you can bucket your candidates who fall into specific experience ranges:

```
$ curl -XPOST http://localhost:9200/hrms/candidate/_search?pretty -d '{
    "aggs": {
      "cand_exp_dist": {
        "range": {
          "field": "experience",
          "ranges": [
            {
              "from": 0,
              "to": 3
            },
            {
              "from": 3,
```

```
            "to": 7
          },
          {
            "from": 7,
            "to": 10
          },
          {
            "from": 10,
            "to": 20
          }
        ]
      }
    }
  }
}'
```

The geo distance

Elasticsearch provides a rich support to perform the computation of geo points. Geo distance aggregation creates buckets of documents in the ranges from the reference location provided in the query.

The following query finds the distribution of candidates around Mumbai with the elasticsearch skill:

```
$ curl -XPOST http://localhost:9200/hrms/candidate/_search?pretty -d '{
  "query": {
    "term": {
      "skills": {
        "value": "elasticsearch"
      }
    }
  },
  "aggs": {
    "around_mumbai": {
      "geo_distance": {
        "field": "address.geo",
        "origin": "18.97, 72.82",
```

```
      "unit": "km",
      "ranges": [
        {
          "to": 200
        },
        {
          "from": 200,
          "to": 500
        },
        {
          "from": 500,
          "to": 1000
        },
        {
          "from": 1000
        }
      ]
    }
  }
},
"size": 10,
"post_filter": {
  "term": {
    "address.city": "Mumbai"
  }
}
}'
```

Notice the use of the term query above as a part of the query parameter. It restricts the list of hits, as well as the input for the calculation of aggregations. You can apply the filter only on the returned hits using post_filter.

Elasticsearch provides Geo hash aggregation that provides the distribution of geo points on the set of documents with a given precision. Geo bounds aggregation can be used to find documents that fall into a specific geo bounding box.

Sub-aggregations

Elasticsearch can provide multidimensional insights into your data (powered by sub-aggregations). Sub-aggregations provide the ability to nest aggregations to any number of levels.

Consider this example: you wish to know the average experience of candidates with different skills in your top five cities. If you are working with SQL, your query would look similar to the the following command:

```
SELECT c.city, s.skill, avg(c.experience)
  from candidate c LEFT JOIN candidate_skills s ON c.id=s.cid
  GROUP BY c.city, s.skill
```

Here is the equivalent Elasticsearch aggregation query to achieve the same thing:

```
$ curl -XPOST http://localhost:9200/hrms/candidate/_search?pretty -d '{
  "aggs": {
    "by_city": {
      "terms": {
        "field": "address.city",
        "size": 5
      },
      "aggs": {
        "by_skill": {
          "terms": {
            "field": "skills",
            "size": 5
          },
          "aggs":{
            "average": {
              "avg": {
                  "field": "experience"
              }
            }
          }
        }
      }
    }
  },
  "size": 0
}'
```

Try it yourself

Let's try to write an Elasticsearch query to perform the following:

Find city-wise average salaries of candidates with 5 to 10 years of experience in at least two of "lucene" or "elasticsearch" or "kibana" or "analytics" technologies.

For your reference, the answer for this exercise is available in the book's source code, available at `https://github.com/vishalbrevitaz/eshadoop/blob/master/ch03/exercise/avg-salary-by-city-request.sh`.

Summary

In this chapter, we discussed Elasticsearch and understood the common types of indexation and search problems that you may encounter. You learned how to interact with Elasticsearch using its REST API to index and retrieve the documents. We looked at the Elasticsearch mapping API. Understanding its data types will help you to leverage data type-specific queries.

You got an understanding of what is inverted index and how Elasticsearch indexes data after tokenizing and filtering input. You learned how to use built-in analyzers and create custom analyzers that meet your use-case requirements.

We explored the Query DSL module of Elasticsearch by walking through various practical examples of Elasticsearch query types. At the end of the chapter, we discussed the power of aggregation with real-world examples in order to leverage the analytic capabilities of Elasticsearch.

So far in the book, you learned how to get the data from HDFS to Elasticsearch. You have seen how to perform exploratory analysis on the data in Elasticsearch by executing various queries and aggregations. As a next step, we will make this analysis process even easier by enabling visualizations on the data through Kibana.

4
Visualizing Big Data Using Kibana

As your data grows, you may want to pull out interesting insights from the data. That's why you are reading this book, isn't it? Visualizations help you see the data graphically by presenting it with different shapes, sizes, and colors. This helps you to find different patterns in your data that can be extremely difficult to find manually. You will learn about Kibana (the visualization tool for Elasticsearch). This allows you to explore your data, visualize it, slice and dice it, and create reusable dashboards that you can share with your colleagues or save for future analysis.

The following topics will be covered in the chapter:

- Setting up the environment
- Discovering data
- Visualizing data
- Creating dynamic dashboards

Setting up and getting started

In order to try out the examples in this chapter, we will set up Kibana as well as the example dataset. Elasticsearch Kibana 4 provides a web interface to search and visualize logs. It is packaged with an embedded web server to get you up and running quickly.

Setting up Kibana

Let's download the latest version of Kibana with the following command:

```
$ cd /opt
$ sudo wget https://download.elastic.co/kibana/kibana/kibana-4.1.0-
linux-x64.tar.gz
```

Next, extract the archive contents to the Kibana directory using the following commands:

```
$ sudo tar -xvf kibana-4.1.0-linux-x64.tar.gz
$ sudo mv kibana-4.1.0-linux-x64 kibana
```

Now, let's make our Kibana server point to our Elasticsearch instance. Open the Kibana configuration file located at /opt/kibana/config/kibana.yml in an editor of your choice. Locate the configurations mentioned in the following code to change the values of port, host, and elasticsearch_url to the values applicable for your setup. The following example shows how it looks in my setup:

```
# Kibana is served by a back end server. This controls which port to use.
port: 5601


# The host to bind the server to.
host: "localhost"


# The Elasticsearch instance to use for all your queries.
elasticsearch_url: "http://localhost:9200"
```

 Kibana stores all its metadata for visualizations and dashboards in its own ES index. You can change the default configuration of kibana_index: ".kibana" to a different value if you wish to run multiple parallel Kibana instances that point to the same ES cluster. This may be helpful if you wish to manage multiple workspaces for different projects that serve different users.

Setting up datasets

Kibana works out of the box for your data in the Elasticsearch index. Before we get started with Kibana, let's grab some datasets that we can use to create visualizations.

We will use the sample dataset that is downloadable from the code repository at `https://raw.githubusercontent.com/vishalbrevitaz/eshadoop/master/ch04/data/consumer_complaints.csv`. This dataset is tailored from the open dataset provided at `http://catalog.data.gov/dataset/consumer-complaint-database`. This dataset contains consumer complaints received about financial products and services in the U.S.

Here are a few sample entries from the dataset:

```
45356,113533,Credit card,,Billing statement,,OH,Web,07/08/12,07/10/12,GE
Capital Retail,Closed with non-monetary relief,Yes,No,40.156514,-84.24213
```

```
45356,318164,Bank account or service,Checking account,Deposits and withdr
awals,,OH,Web,02/17/2013,02/19/2013,Fifth Third Bank,Closed with monetary
relief,Yes,No,40.156514,-84.24213
```

```
45358,686842,Credit card,,Other,,OH,Phone,01/27/2014,02/05/14,Citibank,Cl
osed with explanation,Yes,No,39.986011,-84.48651
```

```
45359,432559,Mortgage,Conventional fixed mortgage,"Loan modification,coll
ection,foreclosure",,OH,Web,06/14/2013,06/17/2013,Bank of America,Closed
with explanation,Yes,Yes,40.053483,-84.35202
```

```
45365,410959,Mortgage,Conventional fixed mortgage,"Loan servicing,
payments, escrow account",,OH,Web,05/19/2013,05/20/2013,Citibank,Closed
with explanation,Yes,Yes,40.284855,-84.15974
```

```
45365,185400,Bank account or service,Checking account,Deposits and withd
rawals,,OH,Phone,11/06/12,11/08/12,Fifth Third Bank,Closed with monetary
relief,Yes,Yes,40.284855,-84.15974
```

These entries correspond to the following CSV format:

```
ZipCode, ComplaintID, Product, SubProduct, Issue, SubIssue, State,
SubmittedVia, DateReceived, DateSent,Company, CompanyResponse,
TimelyResponse, ConsumerDisputed, Latitude, Longitude
```

Try it out

I encourage you to write a MapReduce job to index the dataset into the Elasticsearch note. You need to pay special attention to the type mapping of the fields. The dataset includes various data types for fields, such as `string`, `boolean`, `date`, `geo_point`, and so on. For the `issue` and `subissue` fields, apart from the normally analyzed field, you may want to have `not_analyzed`, enable a full-text search, and have various charts based on the specific `issue` field or the `subissue` field.

For your reference, the MapReduce job and type mapping is included in the book source code. If you were not able to develop the job yourself, you can use the JAR file built from the source code to directly import the data to Elasticsearch. Ensure that you have imported the file to HDFS and run the MapReduce job to get the data to the Elasticsearch index before continuing with further sections.

Getting started with Kibana

Now that we have configured Kibana and imported the dataset to our Elasticsearch instance, we are ready to start the Kibana server with the following command:

```
$ /opt/kibana/bin/kibana
```

Soon after executing this command, you can click on the URL in your browser. In the default configuration, it should be available at `http://localhost:5601/`. Right after loading, Kibana will ask you to configure the index and the time field to be used for the data discovery and visualizations.

The following image shows the index configuration screen of Kibana:

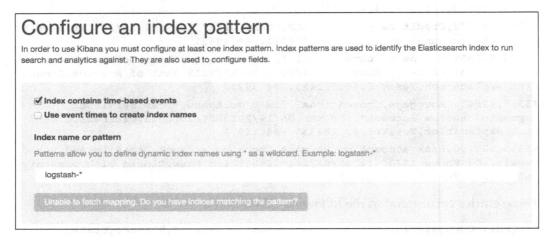

As shown in the preceding screenshot, point your Kibana to the `esh_complaints` index and use `dateSent` as the time field.

> If you used the rolling index names for your indexes, you can use wildcard characters (such as `esh_complaints*`) to configure all the indexes that match the pattern, and Kibana will treat the data in all these indexes to show a consolidated view of your data.

Discovering data

Now that we have the Elasticsearch index configured with Kibana, before we get into visualizations, let's explore Kibana and the data that we have indexed into Elasticsearch.

Kibana provides easy-to-use ways to take a quick look at the data. It allows you to filter data with the quick time and query filters. These query filters accept the Apache Lucene query syntax. To start exploring the data, click on the **Discover** menu from the top menu bar in the Kibana screen.

The following screenshot shows the **Discover** screen with no results:

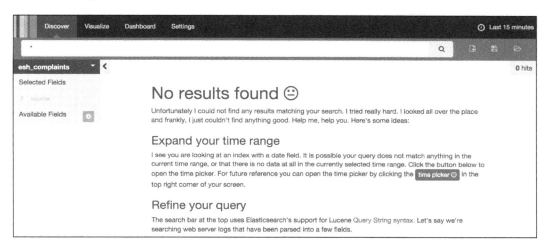

Having said this, can you guess what went wrong? Well, don't worry if you couldn't because it is more likely when you don't have much idea about what's there in the data. Thanks to Kibana developers who can show these nice hints about what could have gone wrong, as shown in the preceding screenshot. The first hint asks you to expand your time range. So, let's try this out with the icon in the top-right corner of the screen to see the options.

The following screenshot shows the time range configuration panel:

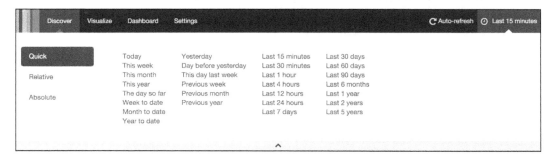

You can choose from the various quick time filters that are available, select a relative filter from current time, or specify the absolute time boundaries. For our data exploration, let's select the **Last 5 years** filter.

The following screenshot shows the **Discover** screen. This shows the all complaints for the last 5 years:

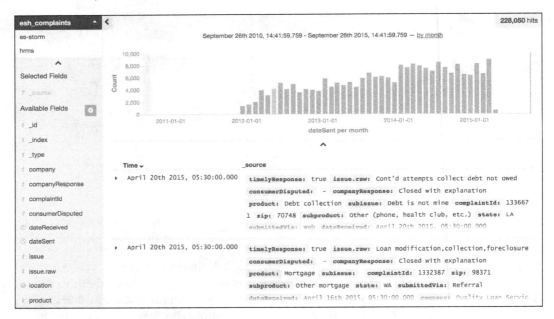

The preceding screenshot shows the monthly distribution of the complaints in the bar chart that represents the date histogram. You can change the distribution unit by clicking on **by month** at the top of the chart. A specific part of the chart can be zoomed in on by clicking or selecting a portion of the chart.

The document's _**source** fields are shown with the **Time** field after the chart. If you want to see only specific fields of the document, you can pick only those fields from the left-hand side bar. You can select and add fields from the available fields to display only those set of fields in the list of the document. You can expand an individual document's row to see all the fields of the document in the tabular or JSON format. In the following screenshot, we will display five important fields in the table. We can see the expanded row to take a look at all the fields.

The following screenshot shows the document fields and values in the form of a table under the **Discover** menu:

If you want to filter the data to show only the documents that relates to loan or mortgage, you can simply enter the text in the text field, as shown in the following screenshot. Kibana will ask Elasticsearch to match the search term against all the fields in the index and show the result with highlighted matches. The chart also updates to reflect the filter we applied.

The following screenshot shows the highlighted search results for the **loan** keyword:

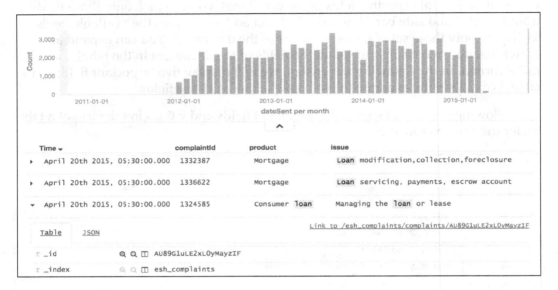

You can use the full-fledged Lucene query in this filter. Here are some quick syntax references that can be handy to explore the data:

- The AND operation on the `issue` field: This specifies `issue:(collect AND debt)`

- The OR operation on the `issue` field: This denotes `issue:( payments OR loan)`

- RANGE on the `dateSent` field: This indicates `dateSent:[01/01/2012 TO 12/31/2012]`

- MUST and MUST NOT: This specifies `(+loan -payments)`

- The fuzzy search to tolerate misspells: This indicates `collectoin~`

You can also save these searches from the search toolbar and use them for future searches.

Visualizing the data

We know how to explore and search our data to get familiar with it. Let's now take a look at how we can answer different questions by giving shape to the data using the visualizations supported by Kibana.

In order to create a new visualization, navigate to the **Visualize** menu to see the range of charts that can be created using Kibana.

The following screenshot shows all the options of visualizations that can be created from the **Visualize** menu:

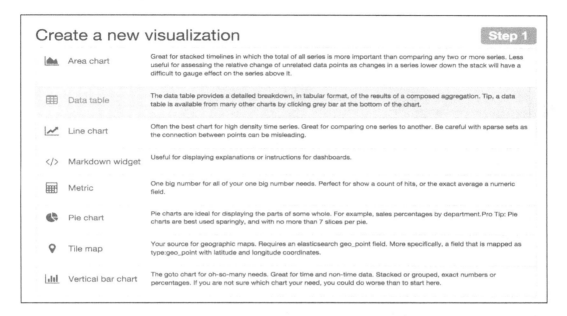

We will take a look at some of these widely used charts from the earlier screenshots to answer our questions and create the dashboard.

The pie chart

Let's start with answering a simple question, that is, which companies have the most number of issues?

Does this kind of question sound familiar from what you learned in the last chapter? Yes, there you go. We can use aggregations to answer such questions, especially the terms aggregation query on the company field to get the top companies with issue count.

We just need Kibana to use the same *terms aggregation* query and prepare a pie chart for us. You can perform the following steps to create this visualization:

1. Click on **Pie chart** in the **Create a new visualization** screen from the previous screenshot.

2. Select **From a new search** from the next screen of the wizard to have the visualization, as shown in the following screenshot.

The following image shows the pie chart created against the _all field:

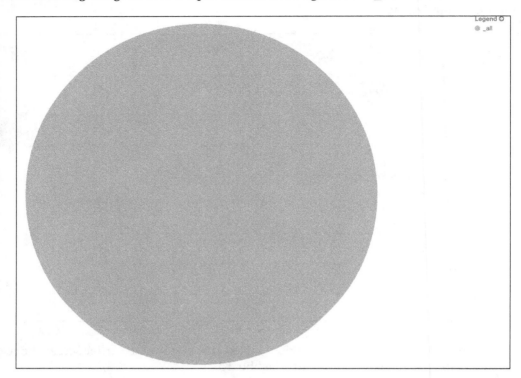

This is not much fun because the chart is plotted against the _all field without any slices. Let's make it better with the following steps:

1. The left sidebar shows the **Data and Options** tab. You may use different metric options, such as Sum, Unique Count, Average, Percentile, and Percentile Rank, based on the field types and the chart type you will work with. Here, we are concerned with just the count metric for the issue, so we will keep the metric unchanged under the **Data** tab.

 Take a look at the **Options** tab to see the possible visual options for the chart. You can enable or disable tooltips and legends as well as convert the pie chart to a donut chart.

2. Under **buckets**, select **Split Slices**.

3. The screen here should show you the options to select the aggregation type; select the **Terms** aggregation.

4. Next, select the `company` field from the field's drop-down list. You can choose to see either the **Top N** or **Bottom N** values by changing the order and size fields.

5. Apply the changes to the chart by clicking on the green button at the top of the left-hand sidebar.

The following screenshot shows the *company-wise issues* in the form of a Pie chart:

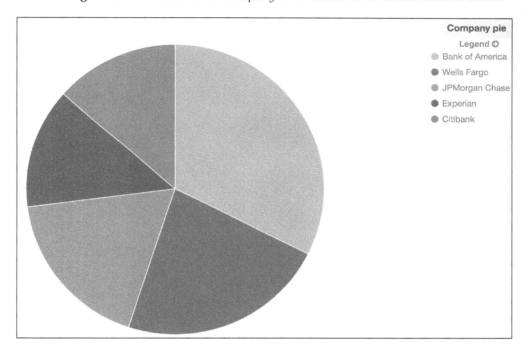

You can expand the bottom bar to view the data in the tabular format, as shown in the following screenshot. You can also see the actual Elasticsearch request, response, and the query execution statistics in the respective tabs.

The following screenshot shows the table view of *company-wise issues*:

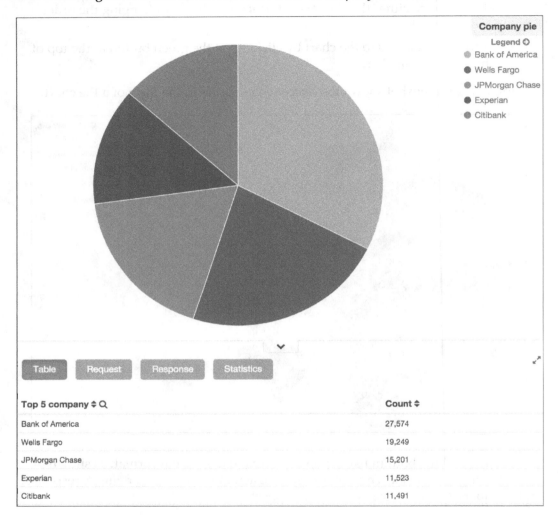

Top 5 company ⇕ Q	Count ⇕
Bank of America	27,574
Wells Fargo	19,249
JPMorgan Chase	15,201
Experian	11,523
Citibank	11,491

The stacked bar chart

Let's take a look at this question: which are the typical issue types reported in the top five companies?

Here, we want to count the top issue types for the top five companies. Can you recall how you can frame your query to get multidimensional data like this one? You are amazing if you got it right. Use sub-aggregations to obtain the stats on multiple dimensions.

Let's generate a chart for the same with the following:

1. First, navigate to the **Visualize** page and click on the **Vertical bar chart**.

2. Just like we did for the pie chart, select the **Terms** aggregation on the company field to map it to the *x* axis.

3. Next, let's click on the **Add sub-bucket** and select **Split Bars**.

4. Now, to create the series for each issue type, select the appropriate issue. raw field with the **Terms** aggregation to generate the chart.

The following screenshot shows the stacked bar chart for the issue types reported by the top five companies:

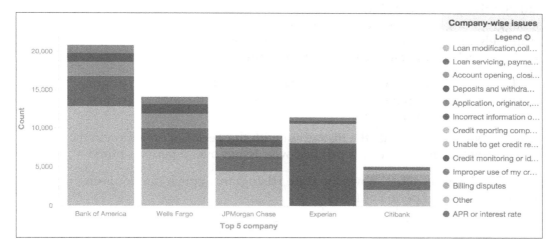

From the preceding screenshot, it is clear that in general, the most common issue type is **Loan modification, collection and foreclosure** for most companies, except **Experian**, which is quite obvious because it deals with credit reporting.

Such multidimensional reports are a great tool to have relative comparisons of different values for two variables in one graph. This makes it easy to understand the patterns in the data.

Let's save the previously generated graph by clicking on the **Save** icon in the search toolbar. We will reuse the same diagram later to add the charts to the dashboard for regular monitoring purposes. Make sure that you save all the upcoming charts that you will prepare so that you can use them when you create the dashboard.

If you don't care about the counts and are only concerned with the proportionate comparison of different values for variables in the *x* axis, you can set the **Bar mode to Percentage** in the **Options** tab.

The date histogram with the stacked bar chart

Let's take a look at another question: how many issues are reported for different products over a period of time?

To answer this question, we need to plot the time and product dimensions. We can do this by using the **Date Histogram** aggregation over the dateSent field and subaggregating it with the **Terms** aggregation in the product field. This can be intuitively projected on a chart by mapping dateSent against the *x* axis and having a series for each product in the bar chart. Perform the following steps:

1. First, create a new vertical bar chart again with the **Date Histogram** aggregation in the dateSent field. You can set the interval, which ranges from **seconds** to **yearly**.

2. Then, subaggregate the histogram with the **Terms** aggregation in the product field to see the product-wise issues over a period of time.

The following screenshot shows the **Date Histogram** aggregation for issues reported for products over a period of time:

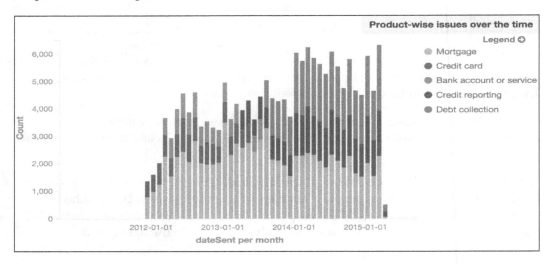

The **Date Histogram** aggregation with the stacked bar chart greatly helps in identifying trends over a period of time on the variable. The preceding screenshot shows that **Debt collection** issues suddenly started around mid-2013, whereas **Bank account and service** issues disappeared from the top issues around the same time.

 It is advisable to limit the number of stacked series in the bar chart to two or three to avoid visual noise in the chart, which makes it difficult to identify the trend quickly.

The area chart

Let's take a look at the following question: how many issues are reported for different states over a period of time?

You may prefer to have an area chart if you are interested in the total value as well, along with the proportion of different values over a period of time. If you just want to have a clear idea about the relative comparison between different series (irrespective of the total), the line chart can be a better visualization.

Irrespective of your specific chart types, you must have seen that Kibana abstracts out the chart-specific complexities and provides you with a uniform way to generate different types of charts. To create an area chart, select it from the **Visualize** screen, and you can follow the similar steps as the previous charts to generate the chart.

The following screenshot displays the issues reported for different states over a period of time in the form of an area chart:

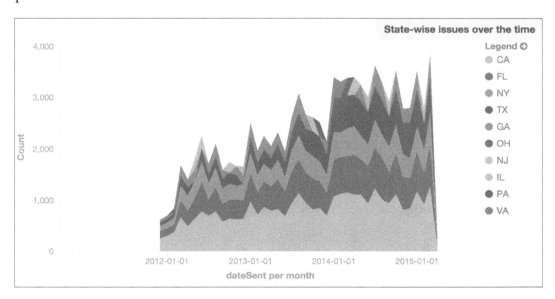

The split pie chart

Let's take a look at the question, how does the proportionate comparison of the top five companies' issue count look for each of the top eight states?

Theoretically speaking, many of the chart types we discussed can be used to visually represent the data to answer the preceding question. However, it is very important to decide the chart type elegantly based on your goal. To clearly show the comparison of the companies for eight different states without interfering with unnecessary details, it may be good to have separate pie charts for each state. Kibana can help you generate such individual charts for each value using the split chart option when you add buckets. Perform the following steps:

1. First, create a new pie chart and add a bucket with the **split chart** option.

2. Here, we wish to split the pie chart for each state, so let's use the **Terms** aggregation on the state field.

3. Add the sub-bucket with **split slices** and the **Terms** aggregation in the company field.

The resulting chart and the split pie chart that shows the comparison for issues reported by the top five companies across the top eight states are shown in the following screenshot:

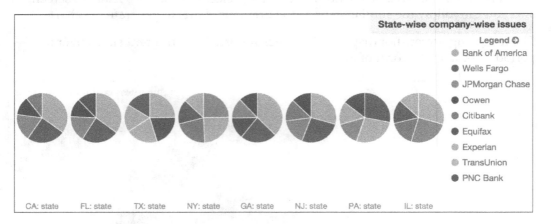

The sun burst chart

Let's take a look at the question, how is the distribution of top products with issues across the top states?

The sun burst chart is a way of representing multidimensional information in the single pie charts. Depending on the applicability and effectiveness of the chart for the use case, this chart can easily go to more than two or even three levels.

You can create a simple sun burst chart similar to the one shown in the following screenshot by creating a pie chart with sub-buckets on the `state` and `product` fields and selecting the **Donut** type from the **Options** tab.

The following screenshot shows the sun burst chart that visualizes the top products with issues across the top states:

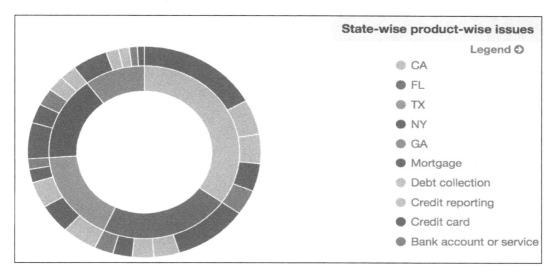

The geographical chart

Let's try to answer another question: how is the distribution of issues across geography?

Kibana supports the visualization of geographical data for the `geo_point` type fields. To try out these geo chart capabilities, create a new visualization with the **Tile Map** type. Select the **Geohash** aggregation type and then the `location` field. The resulting chart is shown in the following screenshot.

The result is calculated using the **Geohash** aggregation. In this case, based on the precision, smaller or larger virtual regions are defined in the map. The documents falling in the same region are aggregated together to derive the count. You can zoom in and out of the map to see the granular-level distribution of issues over the geography.

Geo charts provide various ways to display markers visually. For example, you can select from the heat map, the scaled marker, the shaded circle marker, or the shaded grid. You can change these marker visualizations from the **Options** tab.

The following screenshot shows the heat map visualization of the geographical distribution of issues:

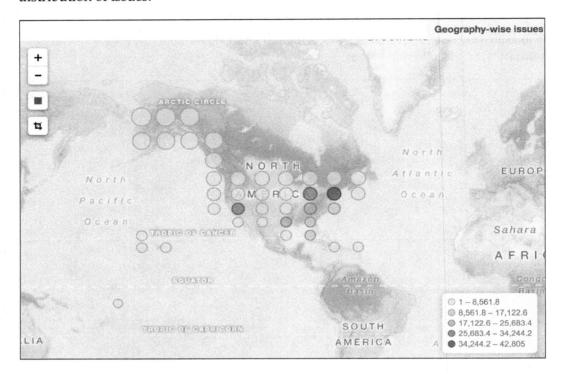

 Apart from these charts, Kibana also supports creating the UI components, such as data tables, markdown widgets, and metric components. These can be used later to add to the dashboard.

Trying it out

You have learned how to find answers to questions related to correlations between different data variables. Exercises are the best ways to learn. Can you try to find what the patterns are for various consumer disputes? Specifically, what are the key observations that affect the likelihood that a consumer disputes? You may want to try out visualizing the `consumerDisputed` field against various variables to find some pattern.

Creating dynamic dashboards

If you need to monitor your charts frequently, it can be quite handy to be able to create a nice dashboard of charts. You can create auto-refreshing dashboards in Kibana by reusing the charts you created before.

To create a new dashboard, perform the following steps:

1. First, navigate to the **Dashboards** link and click on the **New dashboard** button in the toolbar. You should see a blank dashboard.

2. Now, click on the **+** button to add the existing chart to the dashboard.

3. Finally, filter the **Product-wise issues** from the time chart and select it to add it to the dashboard. This will add the chart widget on the screen.

The following screenshot shows the panel to search the visualization to be added to the dashboard:

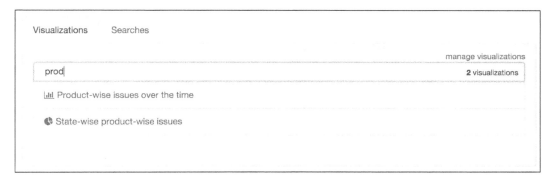

You can resize the widget as per your needs from the icon in the bottom-right corner of the widget by simple dragging it. Similarly, you can add other charts that matter the most to your needs and arrange them on the dashboard.

The following screenshot shows the creation of a sample dashboard with the visualizations we created in the chapter:

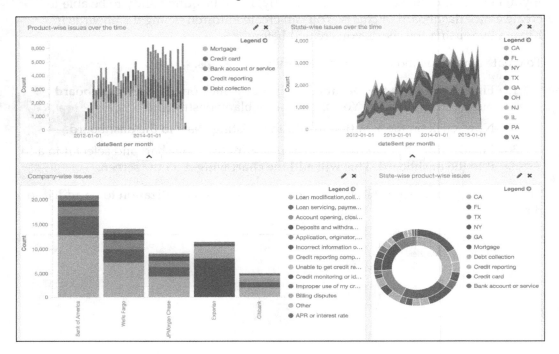

We have bundled the exported JSON file for the dashboard in the source code of the book available at `https://github.com/vishalbrevitaz/eshadoop/blob/master/ch04/setup/complaints-dashboard.json`, which you can import to your Kibana instance in order to have exactly the same dashboard. We will take a look at how to import the exported JSON in a while.

The following screenshot shows the rest of the parts of the same dashboard:

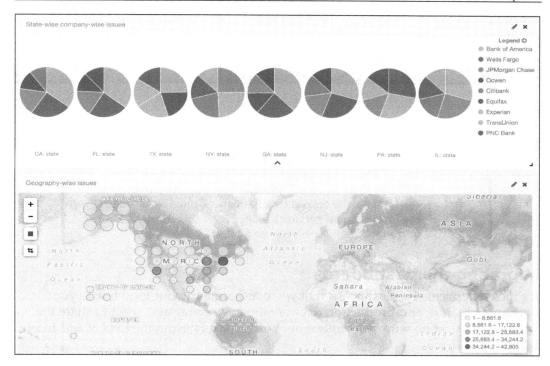

My personal favorite feature of the Kibana dashboard is the global filtering options that get applied to all the charts on the dashboard. All the filtering options that you learned in the *Discovering data* section can be applied here. You can use the Lucene-based query filters and the time filters as well. To try this out, just enter `loan` in the filter box, and the dashboard will update itself to consider only the matched documents.

You can set the **Auto-refresh** interval option for the dashboard if you are planning to monitor the real-time streaming data. You can do this by clicking on the time filter menu at the top to see the **Auto-refresh** option.

The following screenshot shows the panel to select the refresh interval for the dashboard:

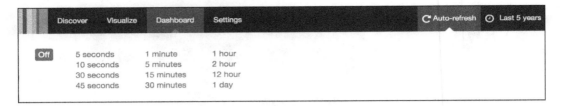

 You can share these dashboards with the respective stakeholders by embedding it on a web page or by sharing the link. You can get quick snippets for this from the **Share** button that is available on the toolbar.

Migrating the dashboards

It's nice to replicate the dashboard that you configured in your local box to your development, test, and production environments. You may also want to share the whole configuration with your colleague. You can do so using the **Export** and **Import** features of Kibana.

In order to export the dashboard configuration, navigate to the **Settings** menu and the **Objects** tab so that you can view the following screenshot. You can export all or only selected dashboards from this screen.

The following screenshot shows how to export or import the Kibana dashboard:

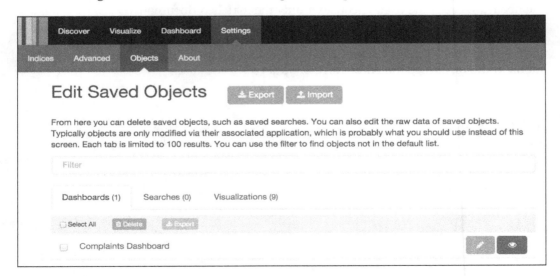

The dashboard gets exported to a nice, human-readable JSON file that can be imported to the target server using the same screen.

Summary

In this chapter, we took a leap forward to explore how to shape up our data. We understood how to quickly explore the data that is indexed in Elasticsearch. We also created different visualizations to see how to slice and dice the data with various charts and find useful insights. You learned how to use pie charts, bar charts, and charts based on time series to visualize the correlation between multiple variables and how to perform exploratory data analysis using Kibana. We created a pretty dashboard for our frequently used charts that can be shared and migrated to a different server.

So far, we covered a full cycle of how to perform analytics on the massive data in your Hadoop filesystem by importing it to Elasticsearch and visualizing it using Kibana. In the next chapter, we will take a look at how Elasticsearch and Apache Storm can be used for real-time analytics. Using real-world examples, we will see how to solve the machine learning problems of *classification* and how data mining problems and *anomaly detection* can be solved using Elasticsearch.

5
Real-Time Analytics

We know how to get interesting insights from the data collected from various sources to the batch mode. However, sooner is always better, especially when it can save you time and money. If there is a threat related to some financial transaction or inventory getting lower, you want to know about such events in a snap, rather than waiting for your nightly jobs to run and your analyst pointing out the threat to you the next morning.

In this chapter, we will take a look at how to import and analyze real-time streaming data in Elasticsearch using Apache Storm. We will also take a look at some of the advanced Elasticsearch functionalities that can be your Swiss army knife in many situations.

The following topics will be covered in the chapter:

- Getting started with Twitter Trend Analyzer
- Injecting streaming data into Storm
- Analyzing the trends in Kibana
- Classifying tweets using percolators

Getting started with the Twitter Trend Analyser

It is best to try out something in order to learn it. This is exactly what we will do in this chapter. So, let's get started by understanding what we are trying to achieve with the examples in the chapter.

What are we trying to do?

Twitter has turned out to be a great voice for users or your customers. Twitter is widely used to recognize trends by analyzing specific keywords or hash tags from the tweets flooding in everyday. In this chapter, we will develop our own Twitter Trends Analyzer using Apache Storm and the capabilities of Elasticsearch. We will bridge these two using ES-Hadoop.

Generally, you would see trend analyzers that provide you with the keywords or hashtags that are in trend, for example, *#elasticsearch* and *#apachestorm* were found to be the trending topics last month. It may be interesting to find out trends at a higher level, for example, **Big Data** was the trending topic last month. Here, when we refer to *Big Data*, we will look up the exact string, but we will group all the *Big Data* ecosystem jargon under one bucket and monitor how the overall trends of *Big Data* looks. Similarly, you can create other categories you're interested in, add keywords or hash tags that are relevant to the category and then analyze the high-level trends. We will use the *classification* technique on the streaming tweet data to tag tweets with matching categories. Moreover, you should be able to view all the trends in different time ranges, such as today, a week, or over the last year.

The following diagram provides a high-level overview of the trend analyzer that we will try to develop:

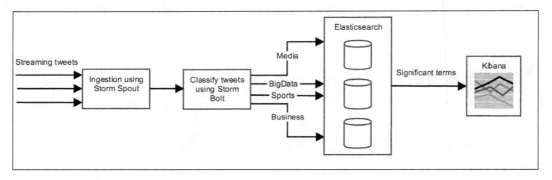

As shown in the preceding diagram, we will receive the stream of tweets in **Storm Spout**; we will classify them into various categories and import them to Elasticsearch. We will then use *significant terms aggregation* to find various trends in Elasticsearch and visualize trends in Kibana. The preceding descriptions may sound quite simple, but identifying trends in a specific dataset out of the huge overall dataset can be a nontrivial task. The same holds true for the *classification*. We will use Elasticsearch *percolators* to solve the classification problem.

Let's set up Apache Storm so that we can use it to receive streaming tweets and push them to Elasticsearch.

Setting up Apache Storm

Apache Storm is a distributed real-time computation engine. It performs the real-time computation of data that Hadoop does in batch mode for batch processing. Here are the steps to set up Apache Storm in the development environment.

Download the required version of Apache Storm with the following command (at the time of writing this book, the latest stable Storm version is 0.9.5):

```
$ cd /usr/local
$ sudo wget http://www.apache.org/dyn/closer.cgi/storm/apache-
storm-0.9.5/apache-storm-0.9.5.tar.gz
```

Extract the archive contents to the `storm` directory using the following commands:

```
$ sudo tar -zxvf apache-storm-0.9.5.tar.gz
$ sudo mv apache-storm-0.9.5 storm
```

Add the storm binaries to PATH by adding the following command to the `~/.bashrc` file:

```
$ export PATH=$PATH:/usr/local/storm-0.9.5/bin
```

We now have Storm ready to use in the local mode. If you wish to set up Storm for production environments in the clustered mode, you may want to set up Zookeeper and have a dedicated nimbus and supervisors to run the topologies of Storm.

Injecting streaming data into Storm

Many of you may already be aware of Storm. However, I will introduce Storm very briefly to all who don't know about it.

Storm provides a real-time computation framework to stream data. So, **stream** is a core data abstraction of Storm. It is composed of an unbounded sequence of tuples. A single unit of the streaming data is known as a **tuple** in the Storm terminology.

The worker components of the Storm job are divided into **spout** and **bolt**. **Spout** is a source of streams. **Bolt** can consume multiple streams. It can perform any processing required and may emit new streams. You can interlink a number of spouts and bolts to create a topology. A **topology** is a top-level abstraction that you can submit to the Storm cluster for execution.

The following diagram shows a sample Storm topology that shows the stream flow from source to target:

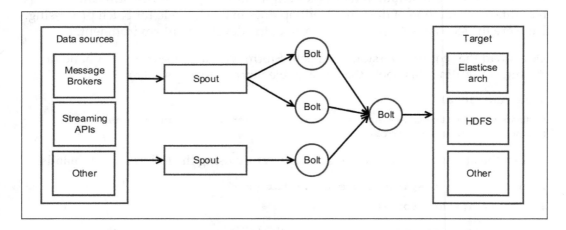

Let's now write our Storm job that will listen to live streaming tweets and inject the fields we want into Elasticsearch. To start with, we will simply listen and dump the required fields from the tweet without performing any classification.

Here is a diagram that shows the topology for a Trend Analyzer:

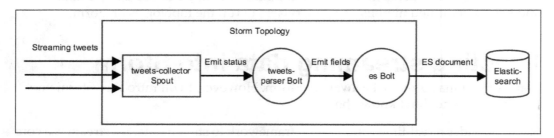

Writing a Storm spout

We will use the Twitter4j API to receive live Twitter streams. Then, we will create a status listener to receive the tweets in the form of the `twitter4j.Status` object.

Here is the relevant code snippet of the listener class that is created as an inner class of the Storm spout:

```java
public class TweetsCollectorSpout extends BaseRichSpout {


    String consumerKey = "<YOUR_KEY>";
    String consumerSecret = "<YOUR_SECRET>";
    String accessToken = "<YOUR_TOKEN>";
    String accessTokenSecret = "<YOUR_TOKEN_SECRET>";
    String[] keyWords = {};
```

In the above code, we created TweetsCollectorSpout by extending BaseRichSpout class provided by Apache Storm. We just initialized required Twitter API credentials. In order to consume Twitter API, you will need to get consumer key and secret by registering the application. Also you need access token key and secret for the twitter app. You can get these credentials from https://dev.twitter.com/.

```java
    SpoutOutputCollector collector;
    LinkedBlockingQueue<Status> queue = null;
    TwitterStream twitterStream;

    @Override
    public void open(Map conf, TopologyContext context,
    SpoutOutputCollector collector) {
        queue = new LinkedBlockingQueue<Status>(1000);
        this.collector = collector;

        StatusListener listener = new StatusListener() {
            public void onStatus(Status status) {
            queue.offer(status);
        }
            ...
            ...
        };
        // Get TwitterStream instance
        // Register StatusListener with TwitterStream
        // Configure OAuth access tokens
        ..
```

To receive the Twitter stream, we need to implement the `StatusListener` interface of the twitter4j API. The `onStatus()` method of `StatusListener` will be called using random samples of tweets generated by users in real time. We initialized the listener when Spout is initialized. You can write your spout initialization code in the `open()` method of `BaseRichSpout`. Moreover, we need a way for Spout's `nextTuple()` method to receive tweets from `StatusListener`. To do this, we will offer each tweet to `LinkedBlockingQueue` and poll it in the `nextTuple()` method. Going further, we will create `TwitterStream` and configure the listener using the stream. We configured the consumer application credentials and the access token using the Twitter stream. The stream provides a random sample of tweets, or we can also filter the stream to match specific keywords. Other methods are not shown in the preceding code snippet because we don't care about these conditions for our purposes in this chapter.

Here are couple of more methods required to get next tuple and declare output fields for next bolt.

```
public void nextTuple() {
    Status status = queue.poll();
    if (status == null) {
        Utils.sleep(50);
    } else {
        collector.emit(new Values(status));
    }
}

public void declareOutputFields(OutputFieldsDeclarer declarer)
{
    declarer.declare(new Fields("tweet"));
}
```

Storm gets the next tuple to process by calling the `nextTuple()` method on the spout. In order to implement the `nextTuple()` method, we will poll the queue to get the status. We called the `emit()` method of the `SpoutOutputCollector` object to pass the status value to get it processed further using the next bolts in the topology. We also need to declare the output field in the `declareOutputFields()` method, as shown in the preceding code snippet. We will just pass the original `status` message in the form of a single `String`, which will be parsed by the next bolt, as shown in the following code:

```
@Override
public Map<String, Object> getComponentConfiguration() {
    Config config = new Config();
    config.setMaxTaskParallelism(5);
    return config;
}
```

You can set task parallelism, as shown in the `getComponentConfiguration()` in the preceding code snippet.

Writing Storm bolts

Storm bolts will receive the tuples emitted by spouts as a single field
tweet. TweetsParserBolt will parse the tweet, extract fields out of it,
and emit fields that can be processed by the next bolt in the topology.

Here is the code of TweetsParserBolt that emits the fields to be processed
by EsBolt:

```
public class TweetsParserBolt extends BaseRichBolt {
private OutputCollector collector;

public void prepare(Map stormConf, TopologyContext context,
OutputCollector collector) {
    this.collector = collector;
}
```

No much is surprising in the preceding code either. We created the
TweetsParserBolt class by extending BaseRichBolt that is provided by Storm.
The prepare() method provides the appropriate OutputCollector instance.

```
@Override
public void execute(Tuple input) {
    ...
    ...
    Status status = (Status) input.getValueByField("tweet");

    String tweet = status.getText();
    String source = status.getSource();
    Date createdDate = status.getCreatedAt();
    HashtagEntity entities[] = status.getHashtagEntities();
    long retweetCount = status.getRetweetCount();
    long favoriteCount = status.getFavoriteCount();
    UserMentionEntity mentions[] = status.
getUserMentionEntities();
    String lang = status.getLang();

// Extract hashtags
    if (entities != null) {
        for (HashtagEntity entity : entities) {
            String hashTag = entity.getText();
            hashtagList.add(hashTag);
        }
    }
    ...
    ...
```

We can override the `execute()` method of `BaseRichBolt` to provide the processing logic of the bolt. In the preceding code, we just extracted the fields of interest from the `Status` object to prepare them to emit to the next bolt.

```
if("en".equalsIgnoreCase(lang)){
        System.out.println("Emitting : " + userHandle+" -> "+
tweet);
        collector.emit(input, new Values(user, userHandle, tweet,
createdDate, location, country, strHashtag, source, lang,
retweetCount, favoriteCount, strUserMention));
    }
```

To avoid noise in our analysis, we will filter out non-English tweets from being indexed in Elasticsearch. Finally, we will emit the values to `EsBolt` so that it can import it to Elasticsearch as an Elasticsearch document. Consider the following code:

```
public void declareOutputFields(OutputFieldsDeclarer declarer) {
        declarer.declare(new Fields("user", "userHandle", "tweet",
                "time", "location", "country", "hashtags",
"source",
                "lang", "retweetCount", "favoriteCount",
"mentions"));
    }
```

As shown earlier, `declareOutputFields()` again declares the fields to be emitted for `EsBolt`.

Creating a Storm topology

As discussed earlier, Storm topologies represent a graph that shows the interconnected spouts and bolts.

Let's create a Storm topology to make our spouts and bolts talk to each other, as shown in the following code:

```
public class Topology {

    public static void main(String[] args) throws
InterruptedException {

        TopologyBuilder builder = new TopologyBuilder();
        builder.setSpout("tweets-collector", new
TweetsCollectorSpout(),1);
        builder.setBolt("tweets-parser-bolt", new
TweetsParserBolt())
                .shuffleGrouping("tweets-collector");
```

In the preceding code snippet, we will set `TweetsCollectorSpout` and `TweetsParserBolt` in the `TopologyBuilder` object. We made the `tweets-parse-bolt` bolt listen to tuples emitted from the specific `tweets-collector` spout with the `shuffleGrouping()` method, as shown in the following code:

```
        Map config = new HashMap();
        builder.setBolt("es-bolt", new EsBolt("es-storm/storm-
tweets",config))
.shuffleGrouping("tweets-parser-bolt")
.addConfiguration(Config.TOPOLOGY_TICK_TUPLE_FREQ_SECS, 2);

        LocalCluster cluster = new LocalCluster();
        cluster.submitTopology("twitter-test", null,
builder.createTopology());
    }
}
```

ES-Hadoop provides a dedicated `EsSpout` and `EsBolt` to get and put data from and to Elasticsearch. In the preceding code, we will configure `EsBolt` to receive tuples from `tweets-parser-bolt`. Finally, we will create a topology instance by calling the `createTopology()` method in the `TopologyBuilder` object. The topology is submitted to the cluster using the `submitTopology()` method.

Building and running a Storm job

We can use Maven configurations and assembly descriptors (similar to those we used in other examples) to build a job JAR file by bundling dependency JARs.

Once you have built the JAR file, you can run the Storm job with the following command. Make sure that Elasticsearch is up and running before executing this command:

```
$ storm jar <PATH_TO_JAR>/ch05-0.0.1-job.jar com.packtpub.esh.streaming.
Topology
```

When you execute the preceding command, it should bootstrap the Storm and Zookeeper servers, start workers, and prepare the spouts and bolts in order to process tweets. A portion of the console output after you start the Storm job is shown in the following code. Soon after this, you should see the stream of tweets printed on the console as well as imported to Elasticsearch, as shown in the following code:

```
16048 [Thread-11-tweets-collector] INFO  backtype.storm.daemon.executor
- Opening spout tweets-collector:(3) 16081 [Thread-13-tweets-parser-
bolt] INFO  backtype.storm.daemon.executor - Preparing bolt tweets-
parser-bolt:(4) 16085 [Thread-13-tweets-parser-bolt] INFO  backtype.
storm.daemon.executor - Prepared bolt tweets-parser-bolt:(4) 16100
[Thread-9-es-bolt] INFO  backtype.storm.daemon.executor - Preparing
bolt es-bolt:(2) 16108 [Thread-17-__acker] INFO  backtype.storm.daemon.
executor - Preparing bolt __acker:(1) 16108 [Thread-15-__system] INFO
backtype.storm.daemon.executor - Preparing bolt __system:(-1) 16116
[Thread-17-__acker] INFO  backtype.storm.daemon.executor - Prepared
bolt __acker:(1) 16120 [Thread-15-__system] INFO  backtype.storm.daemon.
executor - Prepared bolt __system:(-1) 16211 [Thread-11-tweets-collector]
INFO  backtype.storm.daemon.executor - Opened spout tweets-collector:(3)
16213 [Thread-11-tweets-collector] INFO  backtype.storm.daemon.executor
- Activating spout tweets-collector:(3) 16213 [Twitter Stream consumer-
1[initializing]] INFO  twitter4j.TwitterStreamImpl - Establishing
connection. 16982 [Thread-9-es-bolt] INFO  org.elasticsearch.hadoop.
util.Version - Elasticsearch Hadoop v2.1.0.Beta4 [2c62e273d2] 16982
[Thread-9-es-bolt] INFO  org.elasticsearch.storm.EsBolt - Writing to
[es-storm/storm-tweets] 17028 [Thread-9-es-bolt] INFO  backtype.storm.
daemon.executor - Prepared bolt es-bolt:(2) 19823 [Twitter Stream
consumer-1[Establishing connection]] INFO  twitter4j.TwitterStreamImpl
- Connection established. 19823 [Twitter Stream consumer-1[Establishing
connection]] INFO  twitter4j.TwitterStreamImpl - Receiving status stream.
```

Analyzing trends

Once we get the tweets in Elasticsearch, we are ready to start analyzing the tweets using the power of Elasticsearch. In our analysis of tweets, we are mainly interested in trends, as we discussed earlier in the chapter.

In order to perform a trend analysis, it is good to know how we define the trend. A trend is something that is more frequent than usual over a specific time range, location, or field. In other words, it is about knowing what is unusually common. We will essentially try to find some significant changes in normal scenarios.

This process can be seen as an *anomaly detection* as well, in that we will try to find what is it that principally deviates from our overall dataset. We can call this full dataset a *background dataset,* and the dataset we are interested in for a specific time range or location can be called a *foreground dataset.* For example, general occurrences of the word Dornier is about one in 1 million tweets in the background dataset; however, if you take a look at the foreground dataset, that is, tweets today, the word appears five times in 100 tweets. This makes the Dornier word unusually common today.

Significant terms aggregation

Elasticsearch provides out-of-the-box support in order to detect unusually common terms using the significant terms aggregation that we discussed earlier.

Let's create a query to find today's trends from the Twitter dataset that we have collected with the following command:

```
$ curl -XPOST -d http://localhost:9200/es-storm/_search
{
    "size": 0,
    "query": {
        "range": {
            "time": {
                "gte": "now-1d",
                "lte": "now"
            }
        }
    },
    "aggs": {
        "significant_hashtags": {
            "significant_terms": {
                "field": "hashtags",
                "size": 3
            }
        }
    }
}
```

In the preceding query, the range query filters the foreground results. All the entries that exist in the index are considered as a background dataset. You can filter the background dataset using background_filter.

On my machine, the query returns the following response:

```
{
    "took": 31,
    "timed_out": false,
    ...
    ...,
    "aggregations": {
        "significant_hashtags": {
            "doc_count": 42760,
            "buckets": [
                {
                    "key": "ohnoharry",
                    "doc_count": 381,
                    "score": 0.03435635054048922,
                    "bg_count": 381
                },
                {
                    "key": "otrasandiego",
                    "doc_count": 228,
                    "score": 0.018093820892682595,
                    "bg_count": 252
                },
                {
                    "key": "msgblessedbygod",
                    "doc_count": 190,
                    "score": 0.01713308819604449,
                    "bg_count": 190
                }
            ]
        }
    }
}
```

The response returns, doc_count and bg_count, representing the number of entries found in the foreground and background for the term. score represents the ranking that is calculated based on the foreground and background count of the term.

 Significant terms aggregations are typically used as sub-aggregation, making it immensely useful to analyze anomalies by terms, geo location, or ranges.

Viewing trends in Kibana

Let's view the trends generated by our analyzer in Kibana. We will create a bar chart with sub-aggregations to see the trends of today, last week, and last year. Perform the following steps:

1. Navigate to the **Visualize** tab in Kibana and create a new **Vertical bar chart**.
2. For the *X* axis, select the **Date Range Aggregation** in the time field.
3. Add three ranges for today, last week, and last month, as shown in the following image.
4. Add sub-aggregations using **Split Bars** and significant terms aggregation in the hashtags field. You may not see the results as many tweets may not contain hashtags at all.
5. Select the size of four.
6. Go to the **Options** tab and set the **Bar Mode** to **percentage**.
7. Generate the chart.

 In order to generate a meaningful chart (as shown earlier), you will need to run the streaming job for a longer period of time to gather a significant amount of background data. Depending on the amount and range of background data that you may have generated, you can select the relevant range to generate the Kibana chart. For example, to see the trend over last week, you may need to generate data at least for a month or two to see the relevant results.

The following image shows the Kibana chart displaying the trends for the last day, last week, and last month:

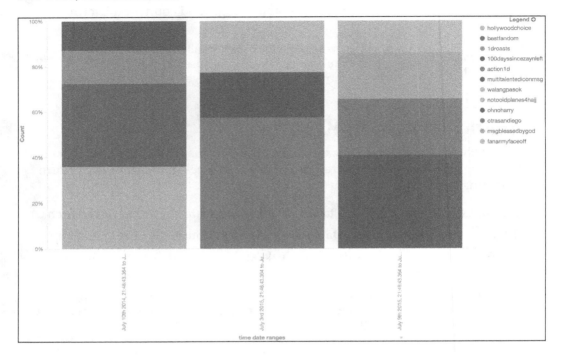

Classifying tweets using percolators

Now, we have a very simple trend analyzer that is already developed. As discussed in the first section of the chapter, we are interested in analyzing trends at a higher level, rather than analyzing them by their hashtags. In this section, we will modify our Storm Bolt to also classify the incoming data in real-time on the fly. To perform the classification, we will take a look at the hashtags of the incoming data and check whether they meet a certain criterion. Based on the this, we will tag the document with the appropriate category.

Percolator

In order to define each criterion for the categorization, we can use the queries of Elasticsearch. When we store the Elasticsearch document, we can check the Elasticsearch queries that match the given document. Percolators are the way to go to achieve this.

Generally, when you search, you have a query that you can execute in the search engine, and the search engine returns the matching documents to you. Percolators reflect the exact opposite of the normal querying process. It means that, when you use a percolator, you have your Elasticsearch queries already indexed. Later, when you have the Elasticsearch document, you can ask the question: Which queries match in the given document?

The following diagram shows how percolators work:

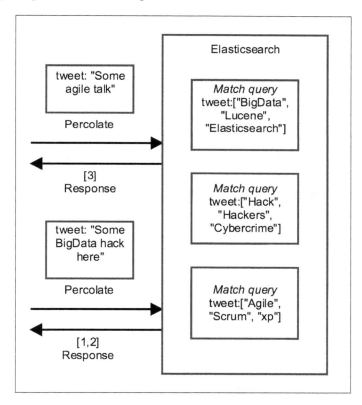

The preceding diagram shows how Elasticsearch already has the matching queries indexed. It defines various criteria's to define categories, such as *Big Data*, *Hacking*, and *Agile*. We can execute the percolate queries against the incoming document, which will be checked against all the queries. The matched queries are passed to the response.

Creating percolator queries is as simple as adding a new query document in the Elasticsearch index. This request will have the Elasticsearch query in the form of a JSON object that will be indexed.

The following command shows how to index a percolator query for the *Big Data* category:

```
$ curl -XPOST 'http://localhost:9200/es-storm/.percolator/1
{
    "query" : {
        "match" : {
            "tweet" : "bigdata analytics hadoop spark elasticsearch
eshadoop nosql mongo mongodb cassandra hbase titan orientdb neo4j storm
pig hive cloudera hortonworks"
        }
    }
}'
```

When you execute the preceding command, it creates a new percolator that contains a query matching any of the *Big Data* ecosystem words specified in the query.

The other part of the percolator API is executing a percolate query. This query provides the ability to match the given document with the queries already indexed in the percolator. This means that we need to provide the document itself in the request. Take a look at the following example:

```
$ curl -XGET 'http://localhost:9200/es-storm/storm-tweets/_percolate'  -d
'{
    "doc" : {
        "tweet" : "I can't believe that I can now analyse trends from the
hadoop data in a snap using Elasticsearch-Hadoop."
    }
}'
```

The preceding `_percolate` request matches the document against the percolated queries. The returned results look similar to the following code:

```
{
    "took": 31,
    "_shards": {
        "total": 5,
        "successful": 5,
        "failed": 0
    },
    "total": 1,
    "matches": [
```

```
    {
        "_index": "es-storm",
        "_id": "1"
    }
    ]
}
```

In the preceding results, the `matches` field lists all the percolated query pointers that match the provided document. The `_id` field points to the percolator `id` that we used when you index the percolator.

 The field referred in the percolator query must already exist in the index.

Building a percolator query effectively

Consider the list of terms we used to index a percolation query for the *Big Data* category in the last section. Coming up with the list of terms that falls under the specific category is not self-evident. The best source to find out such terms would be the tweets themselves generated by users. The bad news is that it is not practical to analyze all the tweets manually to find out what *Big Data*-related terms should be added. The good news is that we already know the significant terms aggregation query in Elasticsearch, and we can leverage it to find out all the terms that appear more often with *Big Data* and its related terms in the user tweets. These terms can become suggestions for you to build your percolator query.

Now let us try to answer a question; that is, find the terms that appear most often along with any of the [*bigdata hadoop spark elasticsearch eshadoop nosql*], which otherwise don't appear so often.

Here is the query to find suggested terms for the *Big Data* category:

```
$ curl -XPOST http://localhost:9200/es-storm/storm-tweets/_search -d '
{
  "query": {
    "match": {
        "tweet": "bigdata hadoop spark elasticsearch eshadoop nosql"
    }
  },
  "aggs": {
    "bigdata_suggestions": {
      "significant_terms": {
```

```
        "field": "tweet"
      }
    }
  },
  "size": 0
}'
```

When you perform such an analysis, you will come to know a few other related terms, such as analytics, mining, data warehouse, or ETL. All the suggested terms may surely not be relevant; however, these suggestions can serve as inputs to a tool where manual selection of the terms can be done. This continuous cycle of feeding the suggestions from the last built percolator terms make the system a self-learning one with little human intervention in selecting terms in order to build a percolation query.

Classifying tweets

With percolators, we are now able to know the query that matches a given document. Once we have the id of a matched query, we can map this id to the respective category name in order to classify the tweet and tag it with its matching categories.

Let's implement this classification in the TweetsParserBolt that we created. Here is the ElasticSearchService class that demonstrates the Java API in order to execute the percolate query:

```
public class ElasticSearchService {

    private TransportClient client;

    public ElasticSearchService(){
        Settings settings = ImmutableSettings.settingsBuilder()
                .put("cluster.name", "eshadoopcluster").build();
        this.client = new TransportClient(settings);
        client.addTransportAddress(new InetSocketTransportAddress("loc
alhost", 9300));
    }
```

The preceding code creates the TransportClient Elasticsearch in the constructor that connects to eshadoopcluster:

```
public List<String> percolate(Map map){
    List<String> ids = new ArrayList<String>();
    PercolateRequest request = new PercolateRequest();
    request.indices("es-storm");
    request.documentType("storm-tweets");
    ActionFuture<PercolateResponse> responseFuture =
client.percolate(request.source(map));
```

```
        PercolateResponse response = responseFuture.actionGet();
        PercolateResponse.Match[] matches = response.getMatches();
        for(PercolateResponse.Match match: matches){
            ids.add(match.getId().toString());
        }
        return ids;
    }
}
```

The `percolate()` method creates `PercolateRequest` by passing the document in the form of a `java.util.Map` object. `PercolateResponse` contains the matched query ids for the document.

Now, we can use this `percolate()` method in order to classify tweets, as shown in the following `classify()` method:

```
private String classify(String tweet) {
        StringBuilder categoriesBuilder = new StringBuilder();
        ElasticSearchService service = new ElasticSearchService();
        Map<String, Object> main  = new HashMap<String, Object>();
        Map<String, Object> doc  = new HashMap<String, Object>();
        doc.put("tweet",tweet);
        main.put("doc",doc);
        List<String> ids = service.percolate(main);
        for(String id :ids){
            categoriesBuilder.append(getCategoryName(id)+" ");
        }
        return categoriesBuilder.toString();
    }

public String getCategoryName(String id) {
        switch (id) {
            case "1":
                return "BigData";
            case "2":
                return "Relational Database";
            case "3":
                return "Sports";
            case "4":
                return "Agile";
            case "5":
                return "Business";
            default:
                return "Other";
        }
    }
```

We will add the category field to the documents that are being indexed in Elasticsearch. The classify() method shown earlier takes the tweet text as input and returns the whitespace concatenated category string that contains all the category tags that are detected for the document. This method creates the Map object that corresponds to the JSON document that we used as a body in the percolate query. The ids that are returned from the percolate() method are mapped to the category name in the getCategoryName() method.

You can run the revised Storm job to verify that the newly added documents also contains the field category, which contains the classified categories. You can use the following query to get last week's category trends from the tweets:

```
$ curl -XPOST -d http://localhost:9200/es-storm/_search
{
  "size": 0,
  "query": {
    "range": {
      "time": {
        "gte": "now-1w",
        "lte": "now"
      }
    }
  },
  "aggs": {
    "significant_categories": {
      "significant_terms": {
        "field": "categories",
        "size": 3
      }
    }
  }
}
```

If you are trying to visualize the category trends in Kibana, you will need to reload the index field list from the Settings page in Kibana to make the newly added fields reflect in Kibana.

Summary

In this chapter, we discussed how to set up Storm to run in the local environment. You learned how to analyze a real-time streaming dataset with the the Twitter Trends Analyzer example. We created the Storm spouts and bolts to get real-time tweets and processed these tweets. We also created the Storm topology to configure our spouts and bolts with ES-Hadoop's EsBolt to inject tweets into Elasticsearch. We explored Elasticsearch's significant terms aggregation query to find the trends and unusually common patterns in the indexed data. We also used percolators to help us classify the documents with stored queries.

In the next chapter, you will understand the important Elasticsearch and ES-Hadoop concepts, such as shards, replicas, data colocations, and advanced configuration options. These concepts and configurations are essential to know before getting your wonderful application into production.

6
ES-Hadoop in Production

So far in the book, we have covered how to utilize the capabilities of ES-Hadoop to make sense of the data in HDFS or from live streaming data. We know how to get data in and out of Elasticsearch and how to execute complex queries on it. However, we didn't need to explore the details of setting up clusters, shards, or replicas. This is how Elasticsearch was intended to be. Elasticsearch makes it so easy to get started and has defaults that make lot of sense in almost all situations. You don't really need to go into detailed configuration if you are not deploying in the production environment.

This chapter will touch important concepts, configurations, and guidelines for Elasticsearch and ES-Hadoop that are essential to know before designing your strategy for production. We will discuss the following topics in this chapter.

- Elasticsearch in a distributed environment
- The Elasticsearch-Hadoop architecture
- Configuring the environment for production
- Administration of clusters

Elasticsearch in a distributed environment

Scalability can be subjective for every deployment. You may be looking for higher query performance, higher availability, or higher indexing performance. In some cases, for small deployments, it may also be sufficient to just add capacity to the existing node in order to scale to higher performance or more volume. However, there is a limit to how much you can scale using a single machine.

Elasticsearch clusters and nodes

A cluster is a group of servers that functions as a single system in order to leverage parallel processing and make the system highly available for its clients. You can simply start multiple Elasticsearch servers with the same cluster name in a dedicated bare metal box or a virtualized environment. These instances will form a cluster. Elasticsearch is designed to provide linear scalability so that in order to achieve more scalability, you can simply add more nodes to the cluster. Elasticsearch has built-in discovery and replication mechanisms, which makes setting up Elasticsearch clusters as easy as starting a new ES instance.

Node types

Each Elasticsearch instance participating in the cluster is termed as a node in the Elasticsearch terminology. By default, all the participating nodes in the cluster store a portion of the data. It can serve incoming user requests. When the search request is received, the nodes that contain different data execute the search query in parallel. These results are then aggregated to provide the final response to the query. The user doesn't need to know the details of which data resides in which node. The cluster provides a unified view of the indexed data, and each node is capable of serving the user request by coordinating with other nodes.

Logically, the Elasticsearch node can be divided into four types based on its responsibilities.

The master node

One of the nodes in the Elasticsearch cluster gets elected as a **master node**. This node possesses a special operational responsibility of coordinating for cluster-wide changes, such as managing indices and mappings, adding or removing nodes from the cluster, reallocating shards, and balancing. This is just an extra responsibility assigned to any one node by default. This is not a heavy workload for bigger clusters. However, it may be desirable to have multiple master nodes to avoid data corruption and an indeterministic cluster state that is caused when a network gets split into two. This is known as the *split-brain problem*. We will take a detailed look at this problem and its resolution later in this chapter.

For bigger deployments, you may want to have dedicated master nodes that will not take up the responsibilities of data storage or query processing. Having dedicated master nodes reduces the chance of cluster instability. You can achieve this by configuring the `node.master` and `node.data` options in the `elasticsearch.yml` file with the following code:

```
node.master: true
node.data: false
```

The data node

Data nodes are nothing but nodes that contain a full-fledged Lucene index. It participates in real indexing and querying operations. All the nodes are given the data node responsibility by default.

Dedicated data nodes can be configured as master nodes in a similar way, as shown in the following code:

```
node.master: false
node.data: true
```

The client node

Client nodes are load balancers that take up the overhead of HTTP requests that parse and delegate requests to data nodes. Thus, client nodes free data nodes and master nodes from extra responsibilities. The client node is also capable of directly redirecting requests to the relevant data nodes. They perform coordination tasks for query execution purposes. They also combine the query results retrieved from each participating node and construct the resulting response for the user.

It is not mandatory to have client nodes in the cluster. If you have them, you should have HTTP disabled in all the other nodes so that they would just communicate among themselves using the internal transport protocol of Elasticsearch. You can do so by setting `http.enabled` to `false`.

Client nodes can be configured using the following configuration:

```
node.master: false
node.data: false
```

Tribe nodes

Elasticsearch also supports tribe nodes that work as a bridge between multiple discrete Elasticsearch clusters. They can work as a load balancer between these two clusters. It also provides the client with a single view as if all backed clusters were a single cluster.

Tribe nodes can be configured with the following configurations:

```
tribe.cluster1.cluster.name: cluster1-name
tribe.cluster2.cluster.name: cluster2-name
```

In the preceding configurations, `cluster1` and `cluster2` in the keys represent the connection name of the cluster. Hence, it can be any arbitrary name that is unique for each connection.

Node discovery

As we know, we can create an Elasticsearch cluster just by starting multiple Elasticsearch instances that have the same `cluster.name`. Elasticsearch automatically finds other nodes to be added to the cluster. Elasticsearch nodes know about each other due to the `discovery` module.

By default, Elasticsearch uses the proprietary Zen discovery method to find other nodes and form a cluster. Elasticsearch sends a ping request to other nodes in the network. It can be configured to perform a multicast or unicast discovery. It is well suited for deployments in the cloud environment as well.

Multicast discovery

Multicast discovery is the easiest way to set up the Elasticsearch cluster, which often helps in your development environment. All you need to do is just start multiple Elasticsearch nodes in the same network. They will find each other to form a cluster. When you start Elasticsearch servers with their default configurations, nodes send multicast ping requests to a predefined multicast group and port. Other existing nodes respond to the request to acknowledge their status. If the master node is found, it adds other discovered nodes to the cluster; otherwise, a new master is elected.

You can disable multicast discovery by setting the following configuration:

```
discovery.zen.ping.multicast.enabled=false
```

Unicast discovery

In sensitive environments (such as production), you never want to have surprises such as some random nodes joining the cluster. In unicast discovery, a node is configured with the exact host addresses and ports where it can expect other nodes to be available.

Unicast discovery can be configured as follows:

```
discovery.zen.ping.unicast.hosts: ["node1:9300","node2:9300",
"node3:[9300-9400]"]
```

> Once the node finds another node that is part of a cluster, the cluster information is passed to the node. This means that it is not required to configure each and every node of the cluster in all the configuration files, but it should be good enough so that a node can find the other cluster member node.

Data inside clusters

We know that Elasticsearch stores indexed data across the data nodes that are available. Let's take a look at how the data is physically distributed across data nodes to achieve parallelism and failover.

Shards

The total size of an Elasticsearch index may range in terrabytes or petabytes. As the shard size grows, it may go out of capacity for a single node, or it will impact the performance due to limited parallelization. The indexed data in Elasticsearch is segregated into subsets and indexed in different nodes. A **shard** is a partition of a whole Elasticsearch index that contains a subset of the total indexed Elasticsearch documents. A shard always resides as a single unit in a single node. A shard is nothing but a full-fledged Lucene index.

Elasticsearch provides a unified view of the index that is actually backed by a set of Lucene indices distributed across several nodes in the form of shards. The user doesn't need to worry about understanding which document is part of which particular shard or node. The user can index or query the document to any of the nodes. Whenever the Elasticsearch cluster is queried, all the shards execute the query in parallel, and a single node aggregates the results. Thus, a shard is a unit of parallelism in the query execution. By default, the Elasticsearch index creates five shards.

 Does this mean that it is always good to have very high number of shards? Think about it. If you have more shards, you may see a performance gain for querying purposes only if each shard resides in a separate node. As the shard itself is a Lucene index, it does the heavy-duty work whenever it executes the query. If multiple shards reside in the same node, they will compete against the same resources.

Replicas

What happens if a node that contains a shard goes down? Replica comes to the rescue to provide a failover mechanism. You can specify the replication factor for the Elasticsearch index to indicate how many replicas should be available for each shard. For each shard, one copy of the shard is marked as primary shard, whereas others are marked as replicas. Replicas introduce redundancy in the cluster, so if a node with a primary shard dies, one of the replicas of the same shard gets promoted as the primary shard.

Apart from failover, replicas can also participate in search query execution. If the application experiences a huge search traffic load, it makes sense to have more hardware to have dedicated nodes for each shard and replicas to get maximum parallelism. By default, the Elasticsearch index creates one replica of each shard. This setting can be configured when you create an index or with the update index call at a later stage.

You can change the default number of shards and replicas in the **create index** call as follows:

```
curl -XPOST http://localhost:9200/my_index -d '
{
    "settings" : {
        "index" : {
            "number_of_shards" : 10,
            "number_of_replicas" : 2
        }
    }
}'
```

> In the default settings, when you index a document, Elasticsearch makes sure that the document gets indexed in all the replicas. Having a high number of replicas may hamper your indexing performance.

Shard allocation

As nodes are added and removed from the Elasticsearch cluster, the master node decides to relocate the primary and replica shards from one node to another.

We will understand the shard relocation process with a simulated scenario using a small number of nodes that will extrapolate to a higher number of nodes in your production cluster.

The following diagram shows three high-level steps to explain how the shards are initialized and started:

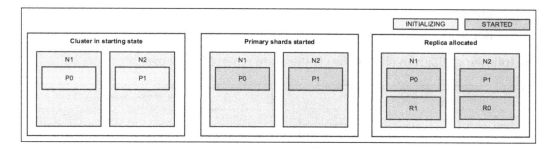

In the Elasticsearch cluster, shards have their own lifecycles. A shard lifecycle consists of four different states: *Unassigned*, *Initializing*, *Started*, and *Relocating*.

Here are the steps showing how the shards are initialized and started as the cluster starts:

- When a cluster starts, both the nodes will initialize the **P0** and **P1** shards
- Soon, both the primary shards are started completely
- Once the primary shards are started, Elasticsearch initializes the replica shards that eventually get started

 Replica shards are allocated in such a way that they do not reside in the same node.

The following diagram shows the state of the cluster when the third node is added:

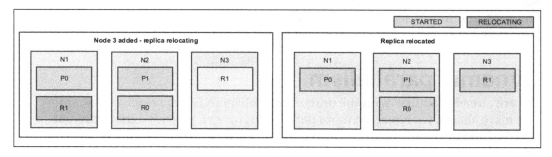

Here are the steps explaining state of shards and replica when third node is added.

- If **Node 3** is added to the clusters, the master node decides to start relocating one of the replicas to the newly added node
- Replicas get successfully started in the new node

The following diagram shows the cluster state when Node 2 dies:

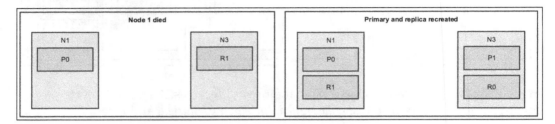

Here are the steps explaining state of shards and replica when Node 2 dies:

- **Node 2** dies, leaving only the primary shard 0 and a replica of shard 1
- **Primary** and **replica** are recreated to make sure that there is one replica of each shard

Elasticsearch performs this relocation to ensure better failure recovery if the nodes die and to ensure maximum parallelism for the query execution.

The ES-Hadoop architecture

We explored the Elasticsearch architecture and the way Elasticsearch achieves scalability in the distributed environment. Hadoop also works in a distributed environment. In this section, we will explore how ES-Hadoop leverages these two distributed systems to combine the capabilities of both systems.

Dynamic parallelism

We are already familiar with the unit of parallelism in Elasticsearch as a shard. The more shards we have, the more parallelism we get, provided that different shards don't compete against the same resources. Similarly, you may be already aware about the fact that a split represents the unit of parallelization in Hadoop. InputSplit represents the data input for one mapper. When we run a Hadoop job, InputFormat divides the input into several InputSplits. This is passed on to individual mapper classes for further processing.

The following image shows how ES-Hadoop makes the clusters of Hadoop and Elasticsearch talk to each other:

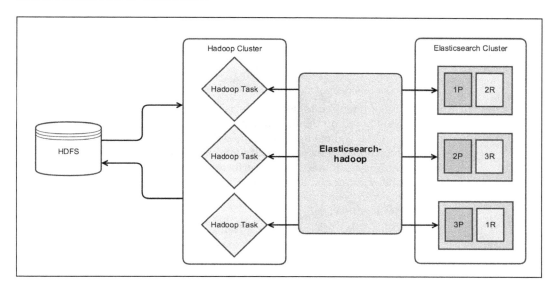

Here, we can see the correlation between the units of parallelism of two systems. The preceding diagram shows that there are two discrete-distributed systems on two sides: Hadoop and Elasticsearch. The Hadoop cluster can have several nodes in it, but only three nodes with Hadoop tasks are highlighted for simplicity. On the other hand, Elasticsearch also has three nodes in the cluster with three shards in it. This has one replica each. Each node or task on one side of the diagram can directly talk to the other node or task. Thus, it provides the peer-to-peer architecture.

ES-Hadoop respects the analogy of splits and shards to enable dynamic parallelism. It means that when you import data from Hadoop to Elasticsearch, ES-Hadoop doesn't just blindly dump the data into any of the Elasticsearch node, but it takes into account the number of shards and divides the indexing request between the available shards. The same holds true when we read the data from Elasticsearch and write it to HDFS using ES-Hadoop.

Writing to Elasticsearch

When you import data from HDFS to Elasticsearch, the input file gets divided into a number of splits and hence and hence into a number of Hadoop tasks. ES-Hadoop then dynamically identifies the number of shards in the target Elasticsearch index and distributes the input data to all the nodes for performing the write operation. A greater number of splits and a comparable number of shards would allow more writes to go in parallel.

Reads from Elasticsearch

When you read data from Elasticsearch to Hadoop, the number of shards drives parallelism. ES-Hadoop infers the shard count in the index. For each shard, it creates the split in Hadoop to leverage the parallelism supported by Elasticsearch. The peer-to-peer mapping of the shard and input split ensures that there is no extra wait time caused because of the unavailability of parallelism from the Hadoop side.

It is not recommended to take the decision about your shard count solely based on the parallelism aspect when you read from Elasticsearch. It is most likely that the default shard count would suffice your needs in most cases. If you must do read optimizations when you import data to HDFS, perform the benchmarks with the default shard count and keep benchmarking with the higher shard count until you get a satisfactory performance. Higher numbers of shards come with a cost.

For benchmarking, you can use the Tsung or JMeter tools. You can start by simulating your production usage pattern. For example, 500 concurrent users performing queries and two indexing jobs indexing 100 documents per second. It will be best to keep the document structure and analyzers that match closely with your real production indices. Measure the performance with such a setup for a few hours for one shard. Do further iterations with more shards to observe how you can increase the shards that affect indexing and query performance.

ES-Hadoop does its best to try to balance the load on different Elasticsearch nodes. It means that, when we execute queries, it takes the round-robin approach to execute queries in different nodes.

Failure handling

When you have large clusters, it is not uncommon to have your nodes encounter network failures or `OutOfMemory` issues. The system must be designed to deal with such failures. ES-Hadoop is not just a client that imports the data to and from Elasticsearch and Hadoop, it also takes care of these network failures as well. If there is a network failure for a node or the node dies, the Elasticsearch cluster still has replicas on the other nodes of the cluster. ES-Hadoop takes this fact into account and finds the replica of the same shard that is least used in recent times and retries the operation in that shard.

Data colocation

ES-Hadoop feeds all the network information and the entire Elasticsearch topology to Hadoop that will interact with Elasticsearch. It performs the colocation, which means that if you have the Elasticsearch server in the same machine as Hadoop or in the same rack, this can save significant amount of bandwidth and make the job run much faster by reducing the amount of data that otherwise would be passed around the network.

Configuring the environment for production

In this section, we will take a look at how to set up the ES-Hadoop cluster in production, and we will see some common deployment best practices, along with some configurations for common production scenarios.

Hardware

Hadoop is known to work with the clusters of commodity hardware. However, when it comes to scale, reliability, and high-performance requirements, Elasticsearch is proven to work way better for medium to large boxes. Also, if you go for a greater number of small boxes, you may just be inviting unnecessary troubles by introducing administration hassles. Although these decisions are highly influenced by budget and project requirements, these are just guidelines that can help you in taking the right decision for your deployments.

Memory

Elasticsearch is known to be memory-hungry. Memory is the first thing that you would like to give to Elasticsearch for good search performance and to avoid OutOfMemory issues, which invites other potential troubles when your nodes die. For production deployments, you should prefer RAM sizes ranging from 16 GB to 64 GB. In the next section, we will take a look at the right configuration and the reasons why so much memory is required.

CPU

Elasticsearch performance isn't impacted much by higher or little lower clock speeds. However, your indexing as well as search performance depends on concurrency, hence the number of threads. Having a greater number of threads makes sense only if you have more underlying cores to allow real parallelism. In production-level clusters, it is best to have four to eight cores. For Elasticsearch, it is best to prefer more cores against a faster CPU if you need to pick one of the two.

Disks

Elasticsearch is IO-intensive for indexing or search requests. IO is even more critical when it comes to systems. This is similar to what we discussed throughout the book, where you will perform lots of bulk imports from HDFS to Elasticsearch. When it comes to high IOPS (input/output per second), SSD disks kick all other spinning disks out of the competition. It is highly recommended to go for SSDs for the production deployments of Elasticsearch.

 You may argue that SSDs are not good at updates and may lead to a shorter life span. But remember that Lucene indices are fully immutable. They perform updates using *mark-as-delete + insert*. Hence, the side effect of update operation goes out of equation when it comes to Elasticsearch and Lucene.

Network

For highly distributed systems that involve the clusters of Elasticsearch and Hadoop, a huge amount of data gets transmitted between different nodes. Having a high-speed network greatly helps in improving the overall system performance and the stability of the cluster by reducing the chances of having network failures between nodes. Always prefer to have all the nodes of your cluster in the same data centers.

Remember to consider the data colocation principal of ES-Hadoop. Pair the Elasticsearch and Hadoop nodes in the same rack to reduce the network latency between the nodes. This greatly improves job performance.

 It is important to have comparable configurations in all the nodes. One may think: I have a couple of machines with 8 GB RAM each, so I should add them to the cluster to increase and add more power and parallelism. This will not be true if you have other machines with way too high configurations (such as 32 GB or 64 GB RAM). Remember that the performance of the cluster will be the performance of the slowest node that participates in the query execution. It may not be a bad idea to use the machines to play other roles (such as the *client* node).

Setting up the cluster

Most of the time, you won't even need to make a single change other than the cluster name in your development environment. However, when you set up the production-level cluster, there are a few essential environment configurations you would like to have in order to save yourself from having a hard time.

The recommended cluster topology

Let's start by taking a look at the topology of a sample cluster that you can use as a reference so that you can modify it as per your needs.

The following image shows a recommended Elasticsearch cluster topology:

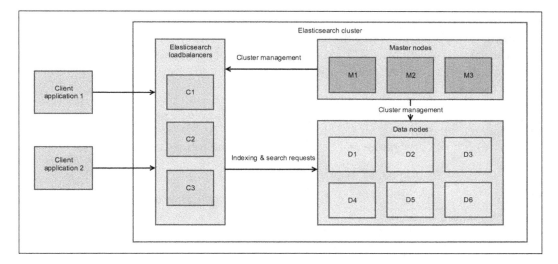

Earlier in the chapter, we discussed about dedicated client nodes, master nodes, and data nodes. As shown in the preceding diagram, the topology leverages the benefits of this division of work responsibility. Client nodes forward the indexing and search requests to data nodes. The master node will interact with the client and data nodes to trigger cluster management tasks.

Having a dedicated responsibility provides you with greater control to troubleshoot and scale your cluster. If you see a high workload from client applications, and if the resource usages are going higher in the client nodes, you can simply add more client nodes. This also improves the stability of each node because they are relieved from additional responsibilities.

The hardware requirements discussed in the previous sections apply mostly to the data nodes of your Elasticsearch cluster. You don't need equally large boxes for master and client nodes. Master nodes have fairly lower resource needs and minimal disk capacity. Client nodes also do not need high disk capacity. They can be small boxes as well.

If you have a limited number of machines, it is not uncommon to combine the responsibilities of master and client nodes with the same nodes. As both of these node types are relatively lighter in weight than data nodes, you will still get pretty good cluster stability with that topology.

Set names

Remember that by default Elasticsearch forms a cluster of nodes in the same network with the same cluster name. The default cluster name is elasticsearch. In production, you must set this cluster name to something different and meaningful in all your cluster nodes.

Most of the configuration in this section applies to the Elasticsearch configuration file under <ELASTICSEARCH_HOME>/config/elasticsearch.yml (unless it is specified otherwise). The cluster name can be changed with the following code:

```
cluster.name: myapp_prod
```

You can have multiple clusters in the same network by configuring a different cluster.name.

It is always good to have a name for each node to troubleshoot postdeployment issues and cluster administration easily. By default, Elasticsearch assigns Marvel superhero names to each node, but they are random and get changed on each server restart. You can set the node names, as shown in the following code:

```
node.name: myapp_es_data_001
```

Paths

By default, Elasticsearch stores data, plugins, and logs in the Elasticsearch home directory. This may cause unintentional deletion when you upgrade the server. I recommend you move your data, plugins, and log directories to a separate directory. Make sure that you provide the required permissions to these directories. Configure these paths as follows:

```
# Configure data directory
path.data: /var/lib/elasticsearch/data
```

```
# Configure plugins directory
path.plugins: /var/lib/elasticsearch/plugins

# Configure logs directory
path.logs: /var/logs/elasticsearch
```

Memory configurations

We already discussed that memory plays a crucial role in Elasticsearch deployments. The default heap size provided to the Elasticsearch node is 1 GB. You would *never* want to miss this configuration for any production deployment. Elasticsearch caches the field data for sorting and faceting for faster performance and filters.

As a best practice, the minimum memory you should assign to the Elasticsearch heap is 50 percent of the total RAM. So, if you have a 32 GB box, assign 16 GB to the Elasticsearch heap. The other half of your memory is not wasted. Lucene uses the OS-level cache out of the Elasticsearch heap size. Lucene leverages the remaining memory to cache segments that are extremely crucial if you perform more of a full text search. Also, it could be utilized by the NIO framework memory, which can be configured in Elasticsearch by configuring the `ES_DIRECT_SIZE` environment variable or through the JVM parameter: `XX:MaxDirectMemorySize`.

> Do not assign more than 30 GB of memory to the Elasticsearch heap. JVM can compress pointers from 64 bit to 32 bit to save memory. If more than around 30 GB of memory is allocated, JVM will use uncompressed pointers that will lead to loss of so losing a lot of memory. If you have got bigger boxes with lots of RAM available in them, you can chose to run multiple Elasticsearch servers in the same machine. This is far more useful for analytics use cases that leveraging Kibana or other dashboarding systems.

You can configure the heap size for Elasticsearch using one of the two methods shown here:

- Set up the `ES_HEAP_SIZE` environment variable in `<USER_HOME>/.bashrc` or the command line with the following command:

  export ES_HEAP_SIZE=30g

- Set up the heap size as JVM arguments when you start Elasticsearch, as shown in the following code:

  ```
  <ES_HOME>/bin/elasticsearch –Xmx30g –Xms30g
  ```

The split-brain problem

In a clustered environment, it is common to have network failures between the nodes; otherwise, the nodes may go out of memory. If the master node suffers such a situation, the remaining nodes in the cluster will carry out the master election process and elect a new master node.

The following image shows how a network split may cause a cluster to transition from the **green state** to the **red state**:

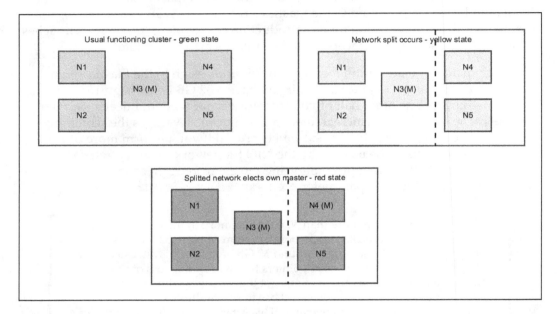

- The preceding image shows the cluster's **green state** when all the nodes are in the network.

- There can be occasions when the network gets divided into two parts, which means that none of the nodes on one side are able to communicate with the other half. This separation of the network is presented in the next block with the **yellow** cluster state, where some of the replica shards are not yet assigned to any nodes. This is just an example scenario. It may happen that the split causes some shards to be lost completely, turning the cluster state to **red**.

- The newly separated network elects its own master as well. In this situation, both the masters perform the cluster management responsibilities that cause the inconsistent state of the index data: data loss. This is represented as a **red** state in the diagram.

You may already know that **green, yellow,** and **red** aren't just colors used in the diagram, they have a special meaning in the Elasticsearch cluster. We will see this in the next section.

It is better to avoid such situations than trying to mitigate the problem later on, which is an extremely difficult task. Elasticsearch supports a configuration called `minimum_master_nodes` to set the minimum number of master nodes that must be available in order to elect a new master node. In the preceding scenario, we could set `minimum_master_nodes` to 3, which means that we carry out the election process only if at least three nodes are available in the network with `node.master` set to `true`. In our case, 3 was a good enough number because it will outright reject the possibility of having three master nodes in any part of the cluster. Thus, it will not allow a new master node to be elected.

A thumb rule to configure `minimum_master_nodes` is shown in the following code:

```
minimum_master_nodes = N/2 + 1
where N = number of nodes eligible to become master i.e. having
node.master = true
```

This can be configured in all the master-eligible nodes, as shown in the following code:

```
discovery.zen.minimum_master_nodes: 2
```

> In case of congested networks, make sure that you set the `discovery.zen.ping_timeout` configuration to a higher value in order to set when the node should be considered to have a network failure.

Recovery configurations

When you restart your cluster after routine maintenance, it may happen that half of the nodes start sooner and the other half start after some delay. When half of the nodes are started, the cluster doesn't find the expected shard distribution in the cluster and tries to rebalance. Just a few minutes later, the rest of the nodes join the cluster to cause another cycle of rebalancing. This results in so much unnecessary data transfer and disk IO in the cluster. The magnitude of this can be extremely high in large clusters with terabytes of data transferring between the nodes.

To avoid this situation, Elasticsearch supports the following configurations:

```
gateway.recover_after_nodes: 3
```

Do not start rebalancing until there are at least three nodes in the cluster:

```
gateway.expected_nodes: 5
gateway.recover_after_time: 5m
```

Start recovery when either the number of nodes in the cluster reaches 5 or after a delay of 5 minutes. The `recover_after_time` configuration doesn't override the `recover_after_nodes` setting. This means that if there are just two nodes waiting for other nodes to join the cluster since 5 minutes, it will not start rebalancing.

Configuration presets

So far, you learned how to configure standard clusters. The standard topology and configurations are good for most use cases. However, there are always exceptions, where there is a possibility of getting an advantage of what is usual for your case.

Rapid indexing

When you use ES-Hadoop, it will automatically optimize the indexing process to perform well. However, there are some additional configurations you can use to check whether it works for your use case.

- Make sure that your input data file generates huge number of `InputSplit` so that you can leverage most of the parallelism for your Hadoop mappers.

- Have peer-to-peer mapping for the Elasticsearch and Hadoop nodes and make sure that each pair is in the closest possible physical proximity.

- Prefer SSD over spinning media.

- For large imports, configure a higher batch size for ES-Hadoop jobs, where the batch size refers to the number of documents that will be sent as part of a single bulk request, as shown in the following code:

```
Configuration conf = new Configuration();
conf.set("es.nodes", "localhost:9200");
conf.set("es.resource", "eshadoop/wordcount");
conf.set("es.batch.size.bytes", "15mb");
conf.set("es.batch.size.entries", "1000");
Job job = new Job(conf, "word count");
```

The highlighted code in the preceding code snippet configures the batch size in terms of bytes and the number of entries for the `word count` job that we created in the first chapter. It executes the batch update whenever any of the mentioned two thresholds is reached.

You can configure `es.batch.write.retry.count` and `es.batch.write.retry.wait` to set the number of maximum retries and the time between each retries.

- Lucene periodically performs segment merging, which consumes lots of I/O. Elasticsearch performs merge throttling in order to ensure that search requests do not suffer. If you don't care about search operations when the indexing job runs, you can disable this using the API call, as shown in the following code (after the job completion, this should be set back to merge):

```
curl -XPUT 'localhost:9200/_cluster/settings' -d '
{
    "transient" : {
        "indices.store.throttle.type" : "none"
    }
}'
```

- If all the indexing operations are triggered from ES-Hadoop jobs, you can set the following configuration in the `elasticsearch.yml` file:

```
index.refresh_interval: -1
```

This configuration will disable the index refresh interval, unless it is called explicitly.

 By default, ES-Hadoop sets `es.batch.write.refresh` to `true`, which means that ES-Hadoop will make an explicit call to refresh the index to make the changes reflect in the search requests.

- Elasticsearch maintains the write ahead logs, also called translogs. These logs help defer the commit until a certain threshold is reached, to ensure atomicity for index and delete operations. Set the translog flush size to a higher value with the following configuration in Elasticsearch:

```
index.translog.flush_threshold_size=1GB
```

- Change `indices.memory.index_buffer_size` to a higher value from its default of 10 percent. It allocates the percentage of memory to be used as an index buffer. Be aware that this will reduce the memory for other operations. Make sure that you benchmark and test it well with your use cases.

- Disable replicas before running jobs with large data. The number of replicas can be changed using the REST API call, as shown in the following code:

```
curl -XPUT 'localhost:9200/{index_name}/_settings' -d '
{
  "index" : {
    "number_of_replicas" : 0
  }
}'
```

 Remember to re-enable the replication back once the job completes. Consider a word of caution: by the time the job executes, there is no replica available for your index.

- Prefer Elasticsearch's autoID if possible. If you generate your own ID, use UUID-1 and the nano time that is similar to an ID. These algorithms generate a zero-padded ID, making it optimized for Lucene.

Lightening a full text search

If most of your use cases are related to a full text search, keep an eye on the following points:

- Use filters over queries wherever possible. Remember that Elasticsearch caches the filter results, not query results.

- When it comes to full text search queries, Lucene has the most role to play. You learned that Lucene caches segments. This takes nonheap memory. You can leave more memory for the operating system. This will be utilized by Lucene to cache the segments, resulting in a superfast full text search.

- Avoid scripts in searches. Scripts act as an enemy of performance.

Faster aggregations

If your Elasticsearch usage is limited to Kibana or similar charting dashboards, you may mostly be using just aggregations.

- Make sure that you provide the maximum ES_HEAP_SIZE possible, within the limit of 30 GB.

- Remember that more shards and replicas on dedicated nodes will enable more parallelism. At the same time, make sure that each shard has a significant size of data to perform aggregations. The accuracy of aggregations can be poor with a small amount of data.

- Check the possibility of filtering the results before performing aggregations. Good candidates for filtering could be fields, such as time range, geography, tenant, and so on.

Bonus – the production deployment checklist

Even for experts, it's pretty easy to miss an important configuration change. Here is a production deployment checklist that you can have as a reference:

- Prefer SSDs, 64 GB RAM, multicore processors, and a lightning fast network.

- Set `ES_HEAP_SIZE` to 50 percent of the total available memory.

- Deploy the topology that leverages the Hadoop and Elasticsearch node colocation.

- Too many shards are not always good. Always benchmark to decide the shard size. Your search queries need to go to each shard before returning the results. If possible, it is always better to use rolling indices that give you an opportunity to change the number of shards later on.

- Configure the cluster name and node names.

- Change data, plugins, and the log file paths so they do not use the Elasticsearch installation directory.

- Create a dedicated client and the master and data nodes, rather than using regular nodes.

- Prefer unicast over multicast.

- Never miss the `minimum_master_nodes` configuration.

- Configure the recovery settings.

- Disable the OS swapping using `sudo swapoff -a` or in `/etc/fstab` for a performance boost.

- Configure the maximum file descriptors in `/etc/security/limit.conf`, as shown in the following code:

```
eshadoop        soft    nofile          64000
eshadoop        hard    nofile          64000
```

- If multiple instances are virtualized in the same machine, use the shard allocation to ensure that each shard doesn't end up in the same physical machine.

- Use configuration management tools, such as Puppet, Chef, and Ansible, to configure your cluster.

- Prefer the default concurrent mark and sweep GC for Elasticsearch. CMS is more mature than Java 8 G1GC. If you change the default GC, I hope that you know what you are doing.

- Avoid tweaking the thread pools. If you do so, do it with caution and consider the number of cores and the thread blocking time to size the thread pool.

- Before trying out further optimizations, make sure that you have done enough benchmarking to prove to yourself that the preceding configurations are not good enough.

- After performing further optimizations; perform benchmarking to verify that the changes make a difference.

- Refer to this checklist before deployment.

Administration of clusters

Once you have deployed your production cluster, it is equally important to monitor the cluster regularly and perform maintenance as required. The Elasticsearch stack supports various APIs to monitor the health of nodes and clusters, along with various tools that make the monitoring task easier.

Monitoring the cluster health

Elasticsearch provides a health API to monitor the health of clusters. Here is an example call and response to obtain the cluster health:

```
$ curl -XGET http://localhost:9200/_cluster/health?pretty
```

This should return the result shown in the following code:

```
{
    "cluster_name": "eshadoopcluster",
    "status": "red",
    "timed_out": false,
    "number_of_nodes": 5,
    "number_of_data_nodes": 5,
    "active_primary_shards": 28,
    "active_shards": 56,
    "relocating_shards": 0,
    "initializing_shards": 0,
    "unassigned_shards": 6,
    "number_of_pending_tasks": 0
}
```

The response shows important information. Many of these metrics in the response are self-explanatory.

Elasticsearch provides three indicators to represent the cluster health:

- **GREEN**: This specifies that everything is all right, and the cluster is fully functional with all the shards and replicas that are allocated.
- **YELLOW**: This indicates that the cluster is properly functioning and all the data is searchable and available. Some of the replicas are not allocated, so if more shards fail, you may lose some data.
- **RED**: This denotes that the cluster is functional, but some data is missing. The query results are not accurate (at least one primary shard is missing).

Some of the other metrics worth noting are explained here:

- `active_primary_shards` and `active_shards`: This represents the total number of primary and total (primary + replica) shards across all indices
- `initializing_shards`: This represents the number of shards that are either being created or being loaded from the disk after restart
- `unassigned_shards`: This indicates the number of shards that could not be assigned to any nodes because of the lesser number of nodes available in the cluster
- `number_of_pending_tasks`: This mentions the number of cluster-level changes that are yet to be executed

The preceding returned result shows the cluster state as **red**. This indicates that something is wrong with the data. We can see that there are six unassigned shards. However, you cannot exactly predict the indices that are fine and the indices that have problems. It can be a problem with a single index or it can span across multiple indices. You need the index-level health to know the exact details. You can get the index-level health metrics by adding the `level` parameter, as shown in the following command:

```
$ curl -XGET  http://localhost:9200/_cluster/health?pretty&level=indices
```

This will return the result as follows:

```
{
    "cluster_name": "eshadoopcluster",
    "status": "green",
    "timed_out": false,
    "number_of_nodes": 5,
    "number_of_data_nodes": 5,
    "active_primary_shards": 28,
    "active_shards": 56,
```

```
        "relocating_shards": 0,
        "initializing_shards": 0,
        "unassigned_shards": 0,
        "number_of_pending_tasks": 0,
        "indices": {
          "esh_network": {
            "status": "green",
            "number_of_shards": 5,
            "number_of_replicas": 1,
            "active_primary_shards": 5,
            "active_shards": 10,
            "relocating_shards": 0,
            "initializing_shards": 0,
            "unassigned_shards": 0
          },
          "es-storm": {
            "status": "green",
            "number_of_shards": 5,
            "number_of_replicas": 1,
            "active_primary_shards": 5,
            "active_shards": 10,
            "relocating_shards": 0,
            "initializing_shards": 0,
            "unassigned_shards": 0
          },
          ".marvel-2015.08.05": {
          "status": "red",
            "number_of_shards": 5,
            "number_of_replicas": 1,
            "active_primary_shards": 4,
            "active_shards": 4,
            "relocating_shards": 0,
            "initializing_shards": 0,
            "unassigned_shards": 6
        }
        ..
        ..


    }
```

If you look at the preceding result, it is clear that the problem just pertains to a single index:.marvel-2015.08.05. This has the red cluster state with six unassigned shards (including one primary).

I would highly encourage you to use monitoring tools (such as Marvel) to take a quick glance at the crucial metrics of cluster, node, and JVM in a single dashboard. Watcher is another tool that can be used for real-time monitoring and alerting of the cluster. It can notify you when the metrics reach a certain configured threshold.

Snapshot and restore

Elasticsearch tries its best to ensure that you do not lose your data during routine restarts, maintenance, and upgrades. As a best practice, you should always have a backup that can be restored if there is loss of data. Even if you are indexing to Elasticsearch from another data source, with the backup you can avoid reindexing terabytes of data.

Backing up your data

Elasticsearch provides a snapshot API to back up your data. Apart from the shared filesystem, you can back up your data to various repository types, such as Amazon S3, HDFS, and Azure Cloud, with the specific plugins for these repository types. We will not go through all of these types because this will increase the scope of the book.

You need to set up a repository before you can create a snapshot for your indices. Create a repository as follows:

```
$ curl -XPUT http://localhost:9200/_snapshot/eshadoop_backup -d '
{
    "type": "fs",
    "settings": {
        "location": "/media/backups/eshadoop_backup"
    }
}'
```

This call should return successfully, as shown in the following code:

```
{
  "acknowledged":true
}
```

If you have an ultra fast network and can tolerate a sudden spike in traffic during a snapshot/restore process you can add the settings for max_snapshot_bytes_per_sec and max_restore_bytes_per_sec and set them to higher values (such as 50 MB or 100 MB). The defaults for these values are 20 MB. These settings are also convenient if you are just backing up in your local filesystem or in a physically mounted drive for your small deployments.

To take the current snapshot of all the indices, execute the following command:

```
$ curl -XPUT http://localhost:9200/_snapshot/eshadoop_backup/
snapshot_080815
```

When you execute this command, it should immediately return the following status:

```
{
  "accepted":true
}
```

This indicates that Elasticsearch has already started backing up the indices.

If you want the command to return only after the snapshot process completes, you can set the wait_for_completion request parameter, as shown in the following command:

```
$ curl -XPUT http://localhost:9200/_snapshot/eshadoop_backup/
snapshot_080815?wait_for_completion=true
```

You can pass comma-separated indices in the JSON body to take a snapshot of only specific indices, as shown in the following command:

```
$ curl -XPUT http://localhost:9200/_snapshot/eshadoop_backup/
snapshot_080815 -d '
{
  "indices": "esh_network, es_storm"
}'
```

You can have information about the snapshots and delete the snapshots using the GET and DELETE HTTP methods in the preceding URLs.

Restoring your data

You can restore the data from the snapshot just by executing the following command:

```
$ curl -XPOST http://localhost:9200/_snapshot/eshadoop_backup/
snapshot_080815/_restore
```

This command should return the accepted status immediately. You can use `wait_for_completion` for the restore operation as well. If the indices being restored already exist and they are open, the restore process will fail. As you can guess, the restore won't include any of the added documents after the creation of the snapshot. Make sure that you close the indices before initiating the restore process, and the closed indices should have the same number of shards as the one being restored.

You can selectively restore the index by specifying the `indices` option.

Take a look at the following example:

```
$ curl -XPOST http://localhost:9200/_snapshot/eshadoop_backup/
snapshot_080815/_restore -d '{
    "indices": "esh_complaints",
    "rename_pattern": "esh_(.+)",
    "rename_replacement": "consumer_$1_old"
}'
```

The preceding example sets only the `esh_complaints` index to be restored. `rename_pattern` uses the regex pattern in brackets ( ). This indicates that the variable string that needs to be matched in the index name. `rename_replacement` defines the new name for the index, where `$1` indicates the corresponding variable detected in the `rename_pattern`. In the preceding example, `esh_complaints` will be restored with the `consumer_complaints_old` name.

> You should include a regular backup-and-restore process right from the beginning. Ideally, the process should be automated using appropriate tooling or scripting. Also, the process should be tested beforehand, rather than trying to recover the data when there is an emergency, or when the data has already been lost.

Summary

In this chapter, we started by understanding how Elasticsearch works in the distributed environment. We understood how Elasticsearch ensures failover and parallelism for near real-time query responses. You learned how ES-Hadoop leverages the topology of Hadoop and Elasticsearch deployments to gain maximum performance and provide failover.

Further, you learned the essentials of production, including the hardware, the cluster topology, and the much recommended configurations for deploying any production cluster. We looked at the advanced configurations for some of the common deployment scenarios. We now have a checklist that can be very handy to take a quick look before any production deployment. Finally, we ended the chapter with a brief overview of how to administer the cluster.

In the next chapter, you will learn the various widely used Hadoop ecosystem technologies, such as Pig, Hive, Cascading, and Spark. We will see how to get the data to and from Elasticsearch with these technologies and ES-Hadoop.

7
Integrating with the Hadoop Ecosystem

Throughout the book, we mainly focused on how to write MapReduce jobs that dump data from HDFS to Elasticsearch and the other way round. We used Elasticsearch queries to get insights out of indexed data. The Hadoop ecosystem does a great job making Hadoop easily usable for different users by providing a comfortable interfacing. Examples of these are Hive and Pig. Apart from these, Hadoop integrates well with other computing engines and platforms, such as Spark and Cascading.

In this chapter, we will take a look at how ES-Hadoop can integrate with these Hadoop ecosystem technologies with equal ease to provide you with all the power that you currently have using Hadoop. The following topics will be covered in the chapter:

- Pigging out Elasticsearch
- SQLize Elasticsearch with Hive
- Cascading with Elasticsearch
- Giving Spark to Elasticsearch
- Elasticsearch on YARN

Pigging out Elasticsearch

For many use cases, Pig is one of the easiest ways to fiddle around with the data in the Hadoop ecosystem. Pig wins when it comes to ease of use and simple syntax in order to design dataflow pipelines, without getting into complex programming. Assuming that you know Pig, we will cover how to move the data to and from Elasticsearch. If you don't know Pig yet, never mind. You can still carry on with the steps and by the end of the section, you will at least know how to use Pig to perform data ingestion and reading with Elasticsearch.

Setting up Apache Pig for Elasticsearch

Let's start by setting up Apache Pig. At the time of writing this book, the latest Pig version available is 0.15.0. You can perform the following steps to set up the same version:

1. Download the Pig distribution using the following command:

   ```
   $ sudo wget -O /usr/local/pig.tar.gz http://mirrors.sonic.net/
   apache/pig/pig-0.15.0/pig-0.15.0.tar.gz
   ```

2. Extract Pig to the desired location and give it a convenient name, as shown in the following code:

   ```
   $ cd /userusr/local
   $ sudo tar -xvf pig.tar.gz
   $ sudo mv pig-0.15.0 pig
   ```

3. Export the required environment variables by appending the following two lines in the /home/eshadoop/.bashrc file:

   ```
   export PIG_HOME=/usr/local/pig
   export PATH=$PATH:$PIG_HOME/bin
   ```

4. You can either log out and relogin to see the newly set environment variables or source the environment configuration with the following command:

   ```
   $ source ~/.bashrc
   ```

5. Start the job history server daemon using the following command:

   ```
   $ mr-jobhistory-daemon.sh start historyserver
   ```

6. You should see the Pig console using the following command:

   ```
   $ pig
   grunt>
   ```

It's easy to forget to start the job history daemon once you restart your machine or VM. You can make this daemon run on startup, or you need to ensure this is done manually.

Now, we have Pig up-and-running. In order to use Pig with Elasticsearch, we must ensure that the ES-Hadoop JAR file is in the Pig classpath.

Let's grab the ES-Hadoop JAR file and import it to HDFS with the following steps:

1. Download the ES-Hadoop JAR file that is used to develop examples in this chapter, as shown in the following command:

```
$ wget http://central.maven.org/maven2/org/elasticsearch/
elasticsearch-hadoop/2.1.1/elasticsearch-hadoop-2.1.1.jar
```

2. Move the downloaded JAR as follows:

```
$ sudo mkdir /opt/lib
```

```
$ sudo mv elasticsearch-hadoop-2.1.1.jar /opt/lib/
```

3. Import the jar to HDFS with the following command:

```
$ hadoop fs -mkdir /lib
```

```
$ hadoop fs -put elasticsearch-hadoop-2.1.1.jar /lib/
elasticsearch-hadoop-2.1.1.jar
```

Throughout this chapter, we will use a crime dataset that is tailored from the open dataset provided at https://data.cityofchicago.org/. This tailored dataset can be downloaded from https://raw.githubusercontent.com/vishalbrevitaz/eshadoop/master/ch07/data/crimes_dataset.csv.

Once you have downloaded the dataset, import it to HDFS at /ch07/crime_data.csv.

Importing data to Elasticsearch

Let's import the crime dataset to Elasticsearch using Pig with ES-Hadoop. ES-Hadoop provides the EsStorage class as the Pig Storage.

1. In order to use the EsStorage class, you need to have registered ES-Hadoop JAR with Pig. You can register the JAR that is located in the local filesystem, HDFS, or other shared filesystems. The REGISTER command registers a JAR file that contains **UDFs (user-defined functions)** with Pig, as shown in the following command:

```
grunt> REGISTER hdfs://localhost:9000/lib/elasticsearch-hadoop-
2.1.1.jar;
```

2. Then, load the CSV data file as a relation using the following command:

```
grunt> SOURCE = load '/ch07/crimes_dataset.csv' using
PigStorage(',') as (id:chararray, caseNumber:chararray,
date:datetime, block:chararray, iucr:chararray,
primaryType:chararray, description:chararray, location:chararray,
arrest:boolean, domestic:boolean, lat:double,lon:double);
```

This command reads all the CSV fields and maps each token in the data with its respective fields to the preceding command. The resulting relation, SOURCE, represents the relation with the Bag data structure that contains multiple Tuples.

3. Now, generate the target Pig relation that has the structure that matches the target Elasticsearch index mapping closely, as shown in the following command:

```
grunt> TARGET = foreach SOURCE generate id, caseNumber, date,
block, iucr, primaryType, description, location, arrest, domestic,
TOTUPLE(lon, lat) AS geoLocation;
```

Here, we need the nested object with the geoLocation name in the target Elasticsearch document. We can achieve this by having a Tuple to represent the lat and lon fields. TOTUPLE() helps us create this tuple. We then assigned an alias called geoLocation to this tuple.

4. Finally, store the TARGET relation to the Elasticsearch index, as shown in the following command:

```
grunt> STORE TARGET INTO 'esh_pig/crimes' USING org.elasticsearch.
hadoop.pig.EsStorage('es.http.timeout = 5m', 'es.index.auto.create
= true', 'es.mapping.names=arrest:isArrest, domestic:isDomestic',
'es.mapping.id=id');
```

We will specify the target index and type to store the indexed documents. The EsStorage class can accept multiple Elasticsearch configurations.

es.mapping.names maps the Pig field name to the Elasticsearch document's field name. You can use Pig's field id to assign the custom _id value for the Elasticsearch document using the es.mapping.id option. Similarly, you can set the _ttl and _timestamp metadata fields as well.

Pig uses just one reducer in the default configuration. It is recommended to change this behavior to have parallelism that matches the number of shards available, as shown in the following command:

```
grunt> SET default_parallel 5;
```

Pig also combines the input splits (irrespective of size). This makes it efficient for small files by reducing the number of mappers. However, this will give performance issues for large files. You can disable this behavior in the Pig script as follows:

```
grunt> SET pig.splitCombination FALSE;
```

When you execute the preceding commands, they will create the Elasticsearch index and import the crime data documents. If you take a look at the created documents in Elasticsearch, you can see that the geoLocation value is an array in the [-87.74274476, 41.87404405] format. This is because, by default, ES-Hadoop ignores the tuple field names and simply converts them to an ordered array. If you wish to make your geoLocation field look similar to a key/value-based object with the lat/lon keys, you can do it by including the following configuration in EsStorage:

```
es.mapping.pig.tuple.use.field.names=true
```

Writing from the JSON source

If you have an input as a well-formed JSON file, you can avoid conversion and transformations and directly pass the JSON document to Elasticsearch for indexing purposes.

You may have the JSON data in Pig as chararray, bytearray or in any other form that translates to a well-formed JSON file by calling the toString() method, as shown in the following command:

```
grunt> JSON_DATA = LOAD '/ch07/crimes.json' USING PigStorage() AS
(json:chararray);
```

```
grunt> STORE JSON_DATA INTO 'esh_pig/crimes_json' USING org.
elasticsearch.hadoop.pig.EsStorage('es.input.json=true');
```

Type conversions

Take a look at the type mapping of the `esh_pig` index in Elasticsearch. It maps the `geoLocation` type to `double`. This is done because Elasticsearch inferred the `double` type based on the field type we specified in Pig. To map `geoLocation` as the `geo_point` type, you must create the Elasticsearch mapping for it manually before you execute the script.

 Although Elasticsearch provides the detection of a data type based on the type of a field in the incoming document, it is always good to create type mapping beforehand in Elasticsearch. This is a one-time activity that you should do. Then, you can run the MapReduce, Pig, Hive, Cascading, or Spark jobs multiple times. This will avoid any surprises in the detection of types.

For your reference, here is a list of some of the field types of Pig and Elasticsearch that map to each other. The following table doesn't list no-brainer and absolutely intuitive type mappings:

Pig type	Elasticsearch type
`chararray`	This specifies a string
`bytearray`	This indicates binary
`tuple`	This denotes an array (default) or an object
`bag`	This specifies an array
`map`	This indicates an object
`bigdecimal`	This denotes not supported
`biginteger`	This specifies not supported

Reading data from Elasticsearch

Reading data from Elasticsearch using Pig is as simple as writing a single command using the Elasticsearch query.

Here is the code snippet to print tuples that have crimes related to `theft`:

```
grunt> REGISTER hdfs://localhost:9000/lib/elasticsearch-hadoop-2.1.1.jar
grunt> ES = LOAD 'esh_pig/crimes' using org.elasticsearch.hadoop.pig.
EsStorage('{"query" : { "term" : { "primaryType" : "theft" } } }');
grunt> dump ES;
```

When you execute the preceding commands, it will print the tuples Pig console.

SQLizing Elasticsearch with Hive

Hive has held a special place in the Hadoop ecosystem for a long time because it provides a well-known SQL interface to data in Hadoop. Hive is widely used for data warehousing queries to provide summarizations or perform data analysis.

Setting up Apache Hive

Here are the steps to set up Apache Hive 1.2.1:

1. Download the Hive distribution using the following command:

```
$ sudo wget -O /usr/local/hive.tar.gz http://mirror.sdunix.com/
apache/hive/hive-1.2.1/apache-hive-1.2.1-bin.tar.gz
```

2. Extract Hive to the desired location with a convenient name as follows:

```
$ cd /usr/local
$ sudo tar -xvf hive.tar.gz
$ sudo mv apache-hive-1.2.1-bin hive
```

3. Export the required environment variables by appending the following lines in the /home/eshadoop/.bashrc file:

```
export HIVE_HOME=/usr/local/hive
export PATH=$PATH:$HIVE_HOME/bin
export CLASSPATH=$CLASSPATH:/usr/local/hive/lib/*:.
export HADOOP_USER_CLASSPATH_FIRST=true
export HIVE_AUX_JARS_PATH=/opt/lib/elasticsearch-hadoop-2.1.1.jar
```

4. Source the .bashrc file as follows:

```
$ source ~/.bashrc
```

5. Copy the default environment configuration script of Hive using the following command:

```
$ sudo cp $HIVE_HOME/conf/hive-env.sh.template $HIVE_HOME/conf/
hive-env.sh
```

6. Set the Hadoop path by adding the following code in the hive-env.sh file:

```
export HADOOP_HOME=/usr/local/hadoop
```

7. You can see the Hive console using the following command:

```
$ hive
hive>
```

Importing data to Elasticsearch

Hive treats Elasticsearch just as an EXTERNAL TABLE. You can write the INSERT queries to import the data to Elasticsearch.

Here are the steps to import crime data to Elasticsearch using Hive:

1. Create an external table that represents the source CSV file as follows:

```
hive> CREATE EXTERNAL TABLE source (id STRING,
            caseNumber STRING,
            eventDate DATE,
            block STRING,
            iucr STRING,
            primaryType STRING,
            description STRING,
            location STRING,
            arrest BOOLEAN,
            domestic BOOLEAN,
            lat DOUBLE,
            lon DOUBLE)
ROW FORMAT SERDE
'org.apache.hadoop.hive.serde2.OpenCSVSerde' STORED AS
TEXTFILE LOCATION '/ch07';
```

This command reads the input files under /ch07 in HDFS using OpenCSVSerde.

2. Create a target table for crimes that will represent the Elasticsearch index in Hive with the following command:

```
hive> CREATE EXTERNAL TABLE crimes (
            id STRING,
            caseNumber STRING,
            eventDate DATE,
            block STRING,
            iucr STRING,
            primaryType STRING,
            description STRING,
            location STRING,
            arrest BOOLEAN,
            domestic BOOLEAN,
geoLocation STRUCT<lat:DOUBLE, lon:DOUBLE>)
```

```
STORED BY 'org.elasticsearch.hadoop.hive.EsStorageHandler'
TBLPROPERTIES('es.resource' = 'esh_hive/crimes');
```

You can create the Hive STRUCT to map it to the nested Elasticsearch object of geoLocation, as shown in the preceding query. Standard ES-Hadoop configurations, similar to the ones used in Pig, can be configured for Hive in TBLPROPERTIES.

 Hive is case-sensitive, whereas Elasticsearch is not. Hence, ES-Hadoop converts all the field names to lowercase if they are mixed or to uppercase when indexing is performed.

3. Fetch all the entries from the source table and insert them into the crimes table with the following code:

```
INSERT OVERWRITE TABLE crimes
SELECT s.id, s.caseNumber, s.eventDate, s.block, s.iucr,
s.primaryType, s.description, s.location, s.arrest, s.domestic,
named_struct('lat', cast(s.lat AS DOUBLE), 'lon', cast(s.lon AS
DOUBLE))
FROM source s;
```

If the execution of these commands is successful, you should have the crimes data imported to the esh_hive index. If you take a look at the indexed documents closely, you should find that all the field names are lowercased, that is, productType is converted to producttype. The reason for this is that Hive is case-insensitive, whereas Elasticsearch is not. To make the field name conversion predictable, ES-Hadoop converts all the field names to lowercase.

 You can use the es.mapping.XXX pattern to map all the Hive fields using the Elasticsearch document metadata fields, such as id, ttl, timestamp, parent, version, routing, and so on.

Writing from the JSON source

For JSON sources, you can use the es.input.json configuration (as seen in the last section). The mapped table must have only one column as follows:

```
grunt> CREATE EXTERNAL TABLE crimes_json (jsonData STRING)
STORED BY 'org.elasticsearch.hadoop.hive.EsStorageHandler'
TBLPROPERTIES('es.resource' = 'esh_hive/crimes',
            'es.input.json` = 'true');
```

Type conversions

Here is the list of nonobvious field type mappings of Hive and Elasticsearch:

Hive type	Elasticsearch type
void	This specifies null
tinyint	This indicates byte
smallint	This denotes short
bigint	This specifies long
timestamp	This indicates date
struct	This denotes object
map	This specifies object
union	This indicates not supported yet
decimal	This refers to string
varchar	This denotes string
char	This specifies string

Reading data from Elasticsearch

Let's see how we can create a Hive table that maps all `theft` crime-related documents. Perform the following steps:

1. Create an EXTERNAL TABLE that maps the required Elasticsearch query, as shown in the following command:

```
hive> CREATE EXTERNAL TABLE theft_crimes (
    id STRING,
    caseNumber STRING,
    eventDate DATE,
    block STRING,
    iucr STRING,
    primaryType STRING,
    description STRING,
    location STRING,
    arrest BOOLEAN,
    domestic BOOLEAN,
    geoLocation   STRUCT<lat:DOUBLE, lon:DOUBLE>)
STORED BY 'org.elasticsearch.hadoop.hive.EsStorageHandler'
TBLPROPERTIES('es.resource' = 'esh_hive/crimes', 'es.query' =
'{"query" : { "term" : { "primarytype" : "theft" } } }');
```

2. Once you have the table created, you can use the normal SQL queries to get the data from Elasticsearch. This is how you can get the `theft` counts using location:

```
hive> SELECT location, count(*) as noOfCrimes FROM theft_crimes
group by location;
```

Cascading with Elasticsearch

Cascading abstracts out the complexities of MapReduce by providing a platform for data processing in terms of *pipes* and *taps*. This section may be of interest to you if you already use cascading in your projects, or if you are already aware about cascading and wish to integrate it into Elasticsearch. Hence, a basic cascading knowledge is assumed for this section.

ES-Hadoop comes with a dedicated `EsTap` that implements `SourceSink` and `SourceTap` to provide plug points to integrate it into cascading.

Importing data to Elasticsearch

Let's write a cascading job to import data from HDFS to Elasticsearch.

Writing a cascading job

Here is code for the `main()` method that tells you how to cascade a job's driver class:

```
Properties props = new Properties();
props.setProperty("es.mapping.id", "id");
FlowConnector flow = new HadoopFlowConnector(props);
```

ES-Hadoop provides all the standard configurations that you learned earlier are specified in the `Properties` object. The `Properties` object can then be used to construct the `FlowConnector` instance using `LocalFlowConnector` or `HadoopFlowConnector`. In this case, we will create the `HadoopFlowConnector` instance with the following code:

```
Fields inFields = new Fields("id", "caseNumber", "eventDate",
"block", "iucr", "primaryType", "description", "location",
"arrest", "domestic", "lat", "lon");
TextDelimited scheme = new TextDelimited(inFields, false, ",",
"\"");
Tap in = new Hfs(scheme, "/ch07/crimes_dataset.csv");
```

We declared the input fields that map to the sequence of fields in the input CSV file. The TextDelimited scheme provides a way to tokenize the input string. It also supports escaping, as shown in the following code:

```
String expression = "lat + \", \" + lon";
Fields location = new Fields( "geoLocation" );
ExpressionFunction locationFunction = new ExpressionFunction(
location, expression, String.class );
Pipe toEs = new Pipe("to-Es");
toEs = new Each(toEs, locationFunction,Fields.ALL);
```

We created an expression that merges the lat and lon fields. This expression defines how the geoLocation field should look. It is then used to create a field named geoLocation using ExpressionFunction. This function is applied to each tuple flowing in the pipe, as shown in the following code:

```
Fields outFields = new Fields("id", "caseNumber", "eventDate",
"block", "iucr", "primaryType", "description", "location",
"arrest", "domestic", "geoLocation");
Tap out = new EsTap("localhost",9200, "esh_cascading/crimes",
outFields);
    flow.connect(in, out, toEs).complete();
```

The preceding code snippet creates EsTap for the target index with the required output fields. We can then connect the input source and the output sink with the toEs pipe to connect the flow.

Running the job

Now, it is time to run the job in order to get the data into the Elasticsearch index. But wait, we didn't talk about the data type when we wrote the job. It's worth thinking about how Elasticsearch will know about data types. In this case, Elasticsearch will simply try to autodetect the types based on the incoming data. Hence, it is important to take a look at the data first, as shown in the following code:

```
10178221,HY366678,08/02/15 23:58,042XX W MADISON ST,1811,NARCOTICS,POSS:
CANNABIS 30GMS OR LESS,SIDEWALK,TRUE,FALSE,41.88076873,-87.73136165
```

Here, we are interested in the eventDate field. Elasticsearch can autodetect the date data type for the input string that matches the yyyy-MM-dd'T'HH:mm:ss.SSSZZ format. To make it detect the date type for our date format, we will need to create the mapping in advance with dynamic_date_format, as shown in the following command:

```
$ curl -XPUT http://localhost:9200/esh_cascading
$ curl -XPUT http://localhost:9200/esh_cascading/crimes/_mapping -d '{
  "dynamic_date_formats" : ["MM/dd/yy HH:mm"]
}'
```

Assuming that you have already built the job JAR file (as discussed earlier in the book), you can run the job with the following command:

```
$ hadoop jar ch07-0.0.1-cascading-writer-job.jar
```

Reading data from Elasticsearch

Let's see how to use cascading to read the data of Elasticsearch for further processing or how to import it to some other sink.

Writing a reader job

Here is how the main() method of the EsReader job looks:

```
Tap in = new EsTap("localhost",9200, "esh_cascading/crimes",
"{\"query\" : { \"term\" : { \"primaryType\" : \"theft\" } } }");
```

Create the EsTap input that connects to our crimes type of the esh_cascading index. The constructor also accepts a query DSL, where we pass the term query to find the crimes related to theft, as shown in the following code:

```
Tap out = new StdOutTap(new cascading.scheme.local.TextLine());
Properties props = new Properties();
props.setProperty("es.nodes","localhost");
FlowConnector flow = new LocalFlowConnector(props);
```

Create StdOutTap to simply print the incoming data that flows through the pipe on the console. It is needless to mention that we will use this tap with LocalFlowConnector. We can configure a specific ES-Hadoop in the Properties object and pass it to the LocalFlowConnector constructor as follows:

```
Pipe fromEs = new Pipe("search-from-es");
flow.connect(in, out, fromEs).complete();
```

Create the fromEs pipe and connect it to the input source and the output sink in the FlowConnector instance.

Using Lingual with Elasticsearch

Most cascading users are used to working with the cascading extension called Lingual, which provides the ANSI SQL interface for Hadoop data. ES-Hadoop can connect to Lingual as well.

You can register the existing Elasticsearch index and type as a table in Lingual. This enables you to use the lingual shell to execute all supported SQL syntaxes.

It may be interesting to see the various tools available in the Hadoop ecosystem in order to achieve the same effect. This is driven by various aspects, such as the target users of the tool, performance, compliance with standards, and so on. For example, Pig is focused on data flow development, where you want to quickly script the data pipeline without getting into the complexities of MapReduce. Hive, Lingual, and SparkSQL provide the SQL interfacing for Hadoop, along with many others, such as Impala, Apache Drill, Apache Phoenix, and so on. Hive was originated due to the needs of data analysis for SQL-like interfacing and converts the queries to MapReduce jobs. On the other hand, Lingual was more focused on complying with the ANSI standards. It can work on top of nonHadoop stores and leverage the cascading pipelines.

Here are the quick steps to set up Lingual:

1. Download and run the installation script with the following command:

```
$ curl http://files.cascading.org/lingual/1.2/lingual-client/
install-lingual-client.sh | bash
```

2. Export the environment variables by appending the following two lines in the `~/.bashrc` file:

```
export LINGUAL_HOME=/home/eshadoop/.lingual-client
export PATH=$PATH:$LINGUAL_HOME/bin
```

3. Source the `.bashrc` file as follows:

```
$ source ~/.bashrc
```

4. You can see the lingual console by executing the following command:

```
$ lingual shell
```

Here is how the script to register the `esh_cascading/crimes` type with a Lingual table looks:

```
$ export LINGUAL_PLATFORM=hadoop
$ lingual catalog --init
$ lingual catalog --provider --add /opt/lib/elasticsearch-hadoop-
2.1.1.jar
```

First, perform the lingual initialization and register the `es` provider using the ES-Hadoop JAR as follows:

```
$ lingual catalog --schema esh --add
$ lingual catalog --schema esh --stereotype crimes --add --columns id,
caseNumber, eventDate, block, iucr, primaryType, description, location,
arrest, domestic, lat, lon -types string, string, string, string, string,
string, string, string, string, string, string, string
```

Then, create the lingual schema and stereotype for crimes data with the following command:

```
$ lingual catalog --schema esh --format es --add --provider es
$ lingual catalog --schema esh --protocol es --add --provider es
--properties=host=localhost
```

Finally, set the `es` format and the protocol defined in the `es` provider for the `esh` schema as follows:

```
$ lingual catalog --schema esh --table crimes --stereotype crimes -add
esh_cascading/crimes --format es --provider es --protocol es
```

Create the `crimes` table in Lingual that maps to the `esh_cascading/crimes` type.

Once you have mapped the Lingual table to Elasticsearch, you can go to the `lingual shell` and execute the queries as follows:

```
$ lingual shell
0: jdbc:lingual:hadoop> select * from "esh"."crimes";
```

Giving Spark to Elasticsearch

Spark is a distributed computing system that provides a huge performance boost as compared to Hadoop's MapReduce. It works on an abstraction of **RDD (resilient-distributed datasets)**. This can be created for any data residing in Hadoop. Without any surprises, ES-Hadoop provides easy integration using Spark by enabling the creation of RDD from data in Elasticsearch.

Spark's increasing support for integrating various data sources, such as HDFS, Parquet, Avro, S3, Cassandra, relational databases, and streaming data make it special when it comes to data integration. This means that using ES-Hadoop (along with Spark), you can make all these sources integrate into Elasticsearch easily.

Setting up Spark

In order to set up Apache Spark to execute a job, you can perform the following steps:

1. Download the Apache Spark distribution with the following command:

```
$ sudo wget -O /usr/local/spark.tgz http://www.apache.org/dyn/
closer.cgi/spark/spark-1.4.1/spark-1.4.1-bin-hadoop2.4.tgz
```

2. Extract Spark to the desired location with a convenient name, as shown in the following command:

```
$ cd /user/local
$ sudo tar -xvf spark.tgz
$ sudo mv spark-1.4.1-bin-hadoop2.4 spark
```

Importing data to Elasticsearch

To import the crime dataset to Elasticsearch using Spark, let's see how to write a Spark job. We will continue to use Java in order to write Spark jobs for consistency. Here are the driver program's snippets:

```
SparkConf conf = new SparkConf().setAppName("esh-
spark").setMaster("local[4]");
    conf.set("es.index.auto.create", "true");
    JavaSparkContext context = new JavaSparkContext(conf);
```

Set up the `SparkConf` object to configure the Spark job. As always, you can also set most options, such as `es.index.auto.create`, and other configurations that we have seen throughout the book and chapter. Using this configuration, we created the `JavaSparkContext` object as follows:

```
JavaRDD<String> textFile =
context.textFile("hdfs://localhost:9000/ch07/crimes_dataset.csv");
```

Read the crime data CSV file as JavaRDD. Here, RDD is still the type string that represents each line:

```
JavaRDD<Crime> dataSplits = textFile.map(new Function<String,
Crime>() {
    @Override
    public Crime call(String line) throws Exception {
        CSVParser parser = CSVParser.parse(line, CSVFormat.RFC4180);
        Crime c = new Crime();
        CSVRecord record = parser.getRecords().get(0);
        c.setId(record.get(0));
```

```
. .
. .
String lat = record.get(10);
String lon = record.get(11);

Map<String, Double> geoLocation = new HashMap<>();
geoLocation.put("lat", StringUtils.isEmpty(lat)?
null:Double.parseDouble(lat));
geoLocation.put("lon",StringUtils.isEmpty(lon)?null:Double.
parseDouble(lon));
c.setGeoLocation(geoLocation);
return c;
}
});
```

In the preceding code snippet, we called the map() method on JavaRDD to map each of the input lines to the Crime object. Note that we created a simple JavaBean class called Crime that implements the Serializable interface and maps it to the Elasticsearch document structure. Using CSVParser, we parsed each field into the Crime object. We also mapped the nested geoLocation object by embedding the Map in the Crime object. This map is populated with the lat and lon fields. This map() method returns another JavaRDD that contains the Crime objects, as shown in the following code:

```
JavaEsSpark.saveToEs(dataSplits, "esh_spark/crimes");
```

Save JavaRDD<Crime> to Elasticsearch using the JavaEsSpark class provided by Elasticsearch.

> For all ES-Hadoop integrations, such as Pig, Hive, Cascading, Apache Storm, and Spark, you can use all the standard ES-Hadoop configurations and techniques. This includes dynamic/multiresource writes that use patterns (such as esh_spark/{primaryType}) and JSON strings to directly import the data to Elasticsearch.

To control the Elasticsearch document metadata from being indexed, you can use the saveToEsWithMeta() method of JavaEsSpark. You can pass an instance of JavaPairRDD that contains Tuple2<Metadata, Object>, where Metadata represents the map that has the key/value pairs of the document metadata fields, such as id, ttl, timestamp, and version.

Using SparkSQL

ES-Hadoop also bridges Elasticsearch with the SparkSQL module. SparkSQL 1.3+ versions provide the `DataFrame` abstraction that represent a collection of `Row`. We will not discuss the details of `DataFrame` here. ES-Hadoop lets you persist your `DataFrame` instance to Elasticsearch transparently. Let's see how to do this with the following code:

```
SQLContext sqlContext = new SQLContext(context);
DataFrame df = sqlContext.createDataFrame(dataSplits,
Crime.class);
```

Create the `SQLContext` instance with the `JavaSparkContext` instance. Using the `SqlContextSqlContext` instance, you can create `DataFrame` by calling the `createDataFrame()` method and passing the existing `JavaRDD<T>` and `Class<T>`, where `T` is a JavaBean class that implements the `Serializable` interface. Note that the passing class instance is required to infer the schema for `DataFrame`. If you wish to use nonJavaBean-based RDD, you can create the schema manually. The book source code contains the implementations of both approaches for your reference.

```
JavaEsSparkSQL.saveToEs(df, "esh_sparksql/crimes_reflection");
```

Once you have the `DataFrame` instance, you can save it to Elasticsearch using the `JavaEsSparkSQL` class, as shown in the preceding code.

> SparkSQL as well as ES-Hadoop for Spark are rapidly changing APIs. The APIs may change in the coming versions. Refer to the official documentation of ES-Hadoop and SparkSQL to check the APIs supported for the versions you use.

Reading data from Elasticsearch

Here is a code snippet of `SparkEsReader` that finds all the crimes related to `theft`:

```
JavaRDD<Map<String, Object>> esRDD = JavaEsSpark.esRDD(context,
"esh_spark/crimes", "{\"query\" : { \"term\" : { \"primaryType\" :
\"theft\" } } }").values();
for(Map<String,Object> item: esRDD.collect()){
        System.out.println(item);
    }
```

We used the same `JavaEsSpark` class to create RDD with documents that matches the Elasticsearch query.

Using SparkSQL

ES-Hadoop provides the `org.elasticsearch.spark.sql` data source provider in order to read data from Elasticsearch using `SparkSQL`, as shown in the following code:

```
Map<String, String> options = new HashMap<>();
options.put("pushdown","true");
options.put("es.nodes","localhost");
DataFrame df = sqlContext.read()
.options(options)
.format("org.elasticsearch.spark.sql")
.load("esh_sparksql/crimes_reflection");
```

The preceding code snippet uses the `org.elasticsearch.spark.sql` data source to load data from Elasticsearch. You can set the `pushdown` option to `true` in order to push the query execution down to Elasticsearch. This greatly increases the efficiency because the query execution is collocated where the data resides:

```
df.registerTempTable("crimes");
DataFrame theftCrimes = sqlContext.sql("SELECT * FROM crimes WHERE
primaryType='THEFT'");
for(Row row: theftCrimes.javaRDD().collect()){
   System.out.println(row);
}
```

We registered `table` using the data frame and executed the SQL query on `SqlContext`. Note that we need to collect the final results locally to print them in a driver class.

ES-Hadoop on YARN

YARN (Yet Another Resource Manager) is a default resource manager in Hadoop2. You can use YARN to manage resources for external applications as well, such as Elasticsearch, with the ES-Hadoop connector. With the support of ES-Hadoop, YARN can manage resources for the Elasticsearch cluster, such as the number of CPU cores, the minimum and maximum RAM, and the local or network storage (such as HDFS).

At the time of writing this book, support for YARN is still being used for experimental purposes in ES-Hadoop. However, to get a glimpse of how YARN can manage your Elasticsearch clusters, here are some quick steps:

1. Download `elasticsearh-yarn` as follows:

    ```
    $ wget -O /opt/lib/elasticsearh-yarn-2.1.1.jar http://central.
    maven.org/maven2/org/elasticsearch/elasticsearch-yarn/2.1.1/
    elasticsearch-yarn-2.1.1.jar
    ```

2. Then, download the latest Elasticsearch version with Elasticsearch-yarn, as shown in the following command:

```
$ hadoop jar elasticsearch-yarn-2.1.1.jar –download-es download.
local.dir=./downloads es.version=1.6.0
```

3. If you are not fine with the default configurations or want the plugins to be installed, you just need to recreate the Elasticsearch archive that was downloaded in the previous step. For this, you can extract Elasticsearch, edit the elasticsearch.yml file as per your needs, install plugins, and create the archive again.

4. Now, upload the Elasticsearch and Elasticsearch-yarn JAR file to HDFS with the following command:

```
$ hadoop jar elasticsearch-yarn-2.1.1.jar –install-es hdfs.upload.
dir=/apps/elasticsearch
```

```
$ hadoop jar elasticsearch-yarn-2.1.1.jar –install
```

5. Start two Elasticsearch nodes on YARN with 1GB memory each, as shown in the following command:

```
$ hadoop jar elasticsearch-yarn-2.1.1.jar –start containers=2
container.mem=1024
```

6. Check the Elasticsearch service status using the following command:

```
$ hadoop jar elasticsearch-yarn-2.1.1.jar –status
```

You can also check it by navigating your browser to http://hadoop:8088/cluster.

7. Stop Elasticsearch on YARN with the following command:

```
$ hadoop jar elasticsearch-yarn-2.1.1.jar –stop
```

 By default, Elasticsearch on YARN assigns 2 GB of memory per container. If you are trying it out of the box with a really small amount of RAM, the startup may fail. You can add the yarn.nodemanager.vmem-check-enabled and yarn.nodemanager.resource.memory-mb configurations in yarn-site.xml to disable limiting virtual memory and specify the amount of memory to be allocated for a new container request.

Summary

In this final chapter, we looked at the various Hadoop ecosystem technologies. We set up Pig with ES-Hadoop and developed the script in order to interact with Elasticsearch. You learned how to integrate Hive in order to use SQL to write and read data to/from Elasticsearch. We saw how to flow the data through cascading pipes, make it sink to Elasticsearch, and flow it out from the Elasticsearch source. You also learned how to use ES-Hadoop to integrate Elasticsearch into Spark and empower it with a powerful SQL engine: SparkSQL.

We concluded with a small introduction on how to seamlessly integrate Elasticsearch to run it on the YARN resource manager in order to reduce the administration overhead.

Throughout the book, you learned how Elasticsearch empowers you to get a quick insight into your data, which can be in any form in the Hadoop ecosystem, such as HDFS, Parquet, Avro, S3, RDBMS, or streaming data. You can build real-time analytics systems that solve data mining problems, such as anomaly detection or trend analysis on the streaming data. With a crash course on Elasticsearch and Kibana, we turned our *Big Data* into insights. You can use this knowledge to augment data warehouses by adding full-text search and data discovery capabilities to it. You can develop data discovery tools that work on top of your data lake or sophisticated third-party analytics tools, such as Kibana.

Configurations

Similar to Elasticsearch, ES-Hadoop comes with sensible defaults for most purposes. However, you can configure most of its specific behaviors. You can use the configuration options listed in this Appendix in the `configuration` object of your job. You can use these configurations for any of the Hadoop ecosystem integrations, such as MapReduce job, Pig, Hive, Cascading, Spark, or Storm. The following topics in the book guide you on how to pass these configurations.

For your quick reference, here is a list of configurations supported by ES-Hadoop taken from the official documentation at `http://elastic.co`.

Basic configurations

Here are some of the basic configurations:

es.resource

This defaults to `none`.

Specifies the Elasticsearch resource and type where the data is read from or written to. It must be specified in the `<index>/<type>` format, for example, `es.resource=eshadoop/wordcount`.

es.resource.read

This defaults to `es.resource`.

Specifies the Elasticsearch resource and type where the data is read. It is useful when the same job needs to read and write data to different Elasticsearch indices/types, for example, `es.resource.read=eshadoop/wordcount`

es.resource.write

This defaults to `es.resource`.

Specifies the Elasticsearch resource and type where the data is written. It is useful when the same job needs to read and write data to different Elasticsearch indices/ types, for example, `es.resource.write=eshadoop/wordcount`.

es.nodes

This defaults to `localhost`.

Specifies the Elasticsearch nodes that it needs to connect to. By default, it doesn't have to list all the nodes; ES-Hadoop discovers other nodes that are connected to the cluster. However, you can list more nodes to ensure that ES-Hadoop can connect to the cluster if some nodes are down, for example, `es.nodes=localhost` or `es.nodes=localhost:9200`.

es.port

This defaults to `9200`. This setting only applies to the nodes that don't contain a port in the `es.nodes` configuration, for example, `es.port=9200`.

Write and query configurations

Here are the write and query configurations:

es.query

This defaults to `none`; that is, all the data under the Elasticsearch index and type is returned. Specifies the Elasticsearch query that is used when you read data from Elasticsearch, which can be in one of the three forms:

- `uri`: This specifies the query string parameter, for example, `q=category:Inf ormationTechnology`
- `query dsl`: This specifies any Elasticsearch query. For example, consider the following code:

```
{
  "query":
  {
    "match":["InformationTechnology"]
  }
}
```

- external resource: This points to a file that contains the uri or the query DSL, for example, /path/to/query.json

es.input.json

This defaults to false.

Specifies whether the input is already in the json format or not. The json should look similar to the following code:

```
[
  {
    "id": 10178221,
    "caseNumber": "HY366678",
    "eventDate": "08/02/15 23:58",
    "block": "042XX W MADISON ST",
    "iucr": 1811,
    "primaryType": "NARCOTICS",
    "description": "POSS: CANNABIS 30GMS OR LESS",
    "location": "SIDEWALK",
    "arrest": "TRUE",
    "domestic": "FALSE",
    "lat": 41.88076873,
    "lon": -87.73136165
  },
  {
    ..
    ..
  }
]
```

es.write.operation

This defaults to index.

Specifies how the write to Elasticsearch if the ID of the incoming document already exists or doesn't exist in the Elasticsearch index. It can take four different values:

- index: This specifies that a new document is added and the old document is updated
- create: This indicates that a new document is added and throws an exception if a document with the same ID already exists
- update: This throws an exception if the document doesn't already exist and updates it otherwise

- upsert: This denotes that a new document is added and the old document is merged

If an update or upsert write operation is used, the following additional configurations can be applied:

es.update.script

This defaults to none.

Specifies the script that needs to be used in order to update the document.

es.update.script.lang

This defaults to none.

Specifies the script language.

es.update.script.params

This defaults to none.

Specifies the script parameters in the paramName:fieldname or paramName:<CONSTANT> format. It may be a comma-separated list.

es.update.script.params.json

This defaults to none.

If all parameters are constant, they can be specified in the json format. Consider the following example:

```
{
   "param1":1,
   "param2":2
}
```

es.batch.size.bytes

This defaults to 1mb.

Size in bytes for batch writes with the Elasticsearch bulk API. The bulk size is allocated as per the task instance. It means that, if you have five tasks that run with 1mb batch size, you may have 5mb of data getting indexed at the same time in Elasticsearch.

es.batch.size.entries

This defaults to `1000`.

Specifies the maximum number of entries in a batch write when you use the Elasticsearch bulk API. When this is used along with `es.batch.size.bytes`, when either of these two sizes is reached, the batch update is executed. Again, this setting applies to each task.

es.batch.write.refresh

This defaults to `true`. If a refresh should be executed on the completion of a batch write. This can be very useful when you are interested in analyzing the data being indexed in real time.

es.batch.write.retry.count

This defaults to `3`.

Specifies the number of retries for a given batch. The retries are made for rejected data only. A negative value indicates infinite retries.

es.batch.write.retry.wait

This defaults to `10s`.

Indicates the time to wait between two batch write retries.

es.ser.reader.value.class

Defaults depend on whether MapReduce, Cascading, Hive, Pig, Spark, or Storm is used. Specifies the `ValueWriter` implementation to convert objects to JSON.

es.ser.writer.value.class

The defaults depend on whether MapReduce, Cascading, Hive, Pig, Spark, or Storm is used. Specifies the `ValueWriter` implementation in order to convert objects to JSON.

es.update.retry.on.conflict

This defaults to `0`. In a concurrent environment, this configuration can specify the number of retries when a conflict is detected.

Mapping configurations

Most configurations in this section specify how the metadata fields of an Elasticsearch document are mapped to the incoming document.

es.mapping.id

This defaults to none.

If the incoming document contains the field with the configured name, for example, id in the following example, it should be used as _id in the Elasticsearch document. Similarly, configurations are applied to other metadata fields, for example, es.mapping.id=id.

es.mapping.parent

This defaults to none.

Specifies the document field name that maps to _parent. Constants can be specified as <CONSTANT>, for example, es.mapping.parent=item.id or es.mapping.parent=<1>.

es.mapping.version

This defaults to none.

Specifies the document field name that maps to _version. Constants can be specified as <CONSTANT>, for example, es.mapping.version=version or es.mapping.version=<1>.

es.mapping.version.type

This defaults to none. If es.mapping.version is unspecified; otherwise, it is external.

This specifies the value of one of the version types, such as internal, external, external_gt, external_gte, or force.

es.mapping.routing

This defaults to none.

Specifies the document field name that maps to _routing. Constants can be specified as <CONSTANT>.

es.mapping.ttl

This defaults to none.

Specifies the document field name that maps to _ttl. Constants can be specified as <CONSTANT>.

es.mapping.timestamp

This defaults to none.

Specifies the document field name that maps to _timestamp. Constants can be specified as <CONSTANT>.

es.mapping.date.rich

This defaults to true.

Specifies if the Date object should be returned, or if the native string or long type should be returned.

es.mapping.include

This defaults to none; hence all the fields should be included. Comma-separated field names are specified, only these fields will be indexed or read.

es.mapping.exclude

This defaults to none; hence all the fields should be included. Comma-separated field names are specified, these fields will be not be indexed or read.

Index configurations

Here are the index configurations:

es.index.auto.create

This defaults to yes. If set to no, the job fails if the index doesn't already exist.

es.index.read.missing.as.empty

This defaults to no and throws an exception if the index doesn't exist. If this is set to yes, it returns an empty dataset when the index doesn't exist.

es.field.read.empty.as.null

This defaults to yes. Checks whether ES-Hadoop will treat empty fields as null.

es.field.read.validate.presence

This Defaults to warn.

Specifies how ES-Hadoop should react when missing fields are found. It can take one of the following three values:

- ignore: This indicates that no validation is performed
- warn: This specifies that a warn message is logged
- strict: This denotes that an exception is thrown

Network configurations

Here are the network configurations:

es.nodes.discovery

This defaults to true. Specifies whether to discover other nodes in the ES cluster, or how to use the ones specified in es.nodes.

es.nodes.client.only

This defaults to false. Though not recommended, if this is set to true, ES-Hadoop will redirect all the requests through the client node of the cluster.

es.http.timeout

This defaults to 1m.

Specifies the timeout for the HTTP connection to Elasticsearch.

es.http.retries

This defaults to 3.

Specifies the number of retries if the HTTP request fails.
This retry applies to each node that is declared or discovered through the
es.nodes configuration.

es.scroll.keepalive

This defaults to 10m.

Specifies the timeout between scroll queries.

es.scroll.size

This defaults to 50.

Specifies the number of documents returned by each scroll.

es.action.heart.beat.lead

This defaults to 15s. Timeout before which ES-Hadoop informs Hadoop that the task
is still running to prevent a task restart.

Authentication configurations

Here are the authentication configurations:

es.net.http.auth.user

This is the basic authentication username.

es.net.http.auth.pass

This indicates the basic authentication password.

SSL configurations

Here are the SSL configurations:

es.net.ssl

This defaults to `false` and enables the SSL.

es.net.ssl.keystore.location

This specifies the key store location URL or a classpath entry.

es.net.ssl.keystore.pass

This is the set key store password.

es.net.ssl.keystore.type

This defaults to `JKS` and specifies the key store type.

es.net.ssl.truststore.location

This specifies the trusted store location URL or the classpath entry.

es.net.ssl.truststore.pass

This specifies the trust store password.

es.net.ssl.cert.allow.self.signed

This defaults to `false`.

Specifies whether or not to allow self-signed certificates.

es.net.ssl.protocol

This defaults to `TLS`.

Specifies the SSL protocol to be used.

es.scroll.size

This defaults to 50.

Specifies the number of documents to be returned by each scroll.

Proxy configurations

Here are the proxy configurations:

es.net.proxy.http.host

This is the HTTP proxy hostname.

es.net.proxy.http.port

This indicates the HTTP proxy port.

es.net.proxy.http.user

This denotes the HTTP proxy username.

es.net.proxy.http.pass

This is the HTTP proxy password.

es.net.proxy.http.use.system.props

This defaults to yes.

Specifies whether or not to use the system HTTP proxy properties, such as http.proxyHost and http.proxyPort.

es.net.proxy.socks.host

This is the HTTP proxy hostname.

es.net.proxy.socks.port

This specifies the HTTP proxy port.

es.net.proxy.socks.user

This indicates the HTTP proxy username.

es.net.proxy.socks.pass

This denotes the HTTP proxy password.

es.net.proxy.socks.use.system.props

This defaults to yes.

Specifies whether or not to use the system socks proxy properties, such as socksProxyHost and socksProxyPort.

Index

Thank you for buying
Elasticsearch for Hadoop

About Packt Publishing

Packt, pronounced 'packed', published its first book, *Mastering phpMyAdmin for Effective MySQL Management*, in April 2004, and subsequently continued to specialize in publishing highly focused books on specific technologies and solutions.

Our books and publications share the experiences of your fellow IT professionals in adapting and customizing today's systems, applications, and frameworks. Our solution-based books give you the knowledge and power to customize the software and technologies you're using to get the job done. Packt books are more specific and less general than the IT books you have seen in the past. Our unique business model allows us to bring you more focused information, giving you more of what you need to know, and less of what you don't.

Packt is a modern yet unique publishing company that focuses on producing quality, cutting-edge books for communities of developers, administrators, and newbies alike. For more information, please visit our website at www.packtpub.com.

About Packt Open Source

In 2010, Packt launched two new brands, Packt Open Source and Packt Enterprise, in order to continue its focus on specialization. This book is part of the Packt Open Source brand, home to books published on software built around open source licenses, and offering information to anybody from advanced developers to budding web designers. The Open Source brand also runs Packt's Open Source Royalty Scheme, by which Packt gives a royalty to each open source project about whose software a book is sold.

Writing for Packt

We welcome all inquiries from people who are interested in authoring. Book proposals should be sent to author@packtpub.com. If your book idea is still at an early stage and you would like to discuss it first before writing a formal book proposal, then please contact us; one of our commissioning editors will get in touch with you.

We're not just looking for published authors; if you have strong technical skills but no writing experience, our experienced editors can help you develop a writing career, or simply get some additional reward for your expertise.

ElasticSearch Cookbook

ISBN: 978-1-78216-662-7   Paperback: 422 pages

Over 120 advanced recipes to search, analyze, deploy, manage, and monitor data effectively with ElasticSearch

1. Write native plugins to extend the capabilities of ElasticSearch to boost your business.

2. Integrate the power of ElasticSearch in your Java applications using the native API or Python applications, with the ElasticSearch community client.

3. Step-by step-instructions to help you easily understand ElasticSearch's capabilities, that act as a good reference for everyday activities.

Mastering ElasticSearch

ISBN: 978-1-78328-143-5   Paperback: 386 pages

Extend your knowledge on ElasticSearch, and querying and data handling, along with its internal workings

1. Learn about Apache Lucene and ElasticSearch design and architecture to fully understand how this great search engine works.

2. Design, configure, and distribute your index, coupled with a deep understanding of the workings behind it.

3. Learn about the advanced features in an easy-to-read book with detailed examples that will help you understand and use the sophisticated features of ElasticSearch.